The Book for Dangerous Women

A Guide to Modern Life

Clare Conville, Liz Hoggard
& Sarah-Jane Lovett

ANANSI
INTERNATIONAL

First published in Great Britain in 2011 by Weidenfeld & Nicolson.

This edition published in 2012 by
House of Anansi Press Inc.
110 Spadina Avenue, Suite 801
Toronto, ON, M5V 2K4
Tel. 416-363-4343
Fax 416-363-1017
www.houseofanansi.com

Distributed in Canada by
HarperCollins Canada Ltd.
1995 Markham Road
Scarborough, ON, M1B 5M8
Toll-free tel. 1-800-387-0117

House of Anansi Press is committed to protecting our natural environment. As part of our efforts, this book is printed on paper that contains 100% post-consumer recycled fibres, is acid-free, and is processed chlorine-free.

16 15 14 13 12   1 2 3 4 5

Library and Archives Canada Cataloguing in Publication

Conville, Clare
The book for dangerous women / Clare Conville, Liz
Hoggard, Sarah-Jane Lovett.

Previous title: Dangerous women.
Also issued in electronic format.
ISBN 978-1-77089-016-9

1. Women — Conduct of life. 2. Women — Psychology.
I. Hoggard, Liz II. Lovett, Sarah-Jane III. Title.

HQ1221.C65 2012   646.70082   C2011-908625-5

Canada Council   Conseil des Arts
for the Arts   du Canada

ONTARIO ARTS COUNCIL
CONSEIL DES ARTS DE L'ONTARIO

*We acknowledge for their financial support of our publishing program
the Canada Council for the Arts, the Ontario Arts Council, and the Government of Canada
through the Canada Book Fund.*

Printed and bound in Canada

'I am because you are.'
– AFRICAN PROVERB

*'If there's a book you
really want to read but
it hasn't been written yet,
then you must write it.'*
– TONI MORRISON

*'If there is one person who is still not free, then I am not;
if there is one person who still suffers from insult and humiliation,
then I do. Do you understand yet?'*
– AI WEIWEI

'Begin anywhere.'
– JOHN CAGE

ABSTRACT THOUGHT

'It would be so nice if something would make sense for a change.'

– ALICE, FROM *ALICE'S ADVENTURES IN WONDERLAND*,

LEWIS CARROL

(v: Lateral thinking)

⚘

ACCEPTING A COMPLIMENT

Accepting a compliment can be extremely hard to do, particularly if you have grown up in an environment of criticism. In fact, it is a skill that may take up to a lifetime to accomplish, but it's extremely important that you do.

The most cherished compliments often come out of context, and in unlikely places, and they can often leave the recipient feeling slightly lost for words. Poor compliment etiquette is when you 'deny' the compliment giver, i.e. you imply that the compliment given isn't actually true, because this means that he or she has to redouble his or her efforts and turns a charming, life-enhancing, generous gesture into slightly tedious, therapeutic reassurance.

The double whammy is that you have also insulted the giver a little. The underlying message being that they are somehow not intelligent enough, perceptive enough, or don't know enough about you to make this call.

So acknowledge the compliment gracefully, a simple but heartfelt 'Thank you' will suffice, and let the truth in about yourself too. Gradually, without becoming vain, you will develop self-acceptance and secret confidence.

(v: Secret confidence, Self-deprecation)

ACCEPTING INVITATIONS

Whether it's a no or a yes to the opening of a biscuit tin it is extremely important that you respond, politely, and in good time, to invitations. Our preferred method of reply is, of course, a handwritten letter, but if this is just totally unrealistic, a text or e-mail to the relevant person will do. If it was a private event such as a supper, a party or a trip to the theatre or something similar, don't forget to write a proper thank-you letter.

(v: Debt, Money matters)

❧

ACCEPTING RESPONSIBILITY
(v: Boundaries, Breaking the rules, Grasping the nettle, Money matters,
Opening brown envelopes)

❧

ADVENTURE
'Adventure is worthwhile in itself.'
– AMELIA EARHART

What do you want to do? Where do you want to go? Until the twenty-first century, with a few notable exceptions – cf. *The Wilder Shores of Love* by Lesley Blanch – adventure was considered to be the province of men in topees. However, the combination of the vote, rising hemlines, two world wars, contraception, inspiring female athletes, the birth of television and sensationally effective extreme weather wear have opened up infinite vistas for all of us. So, without upsetting the whole domestic applecart, the time has come to be adventurous. A shortlist of near-to-home, gutsy, sports activities can help to focus the mind, challenge the body and blow away the cobwebs and the boom in Internet-based companies offering trekking, canoeing, archery, fencing, hiking, falconry, shooting, and riding seems virtually limitless. If you fancy a greater challenge to mind, body and spirit, think about a camping expedition in the Kalahari, a riding holiday in Argentina, a bicycling trip through Cambodia and Vietnam, or charity work in Malawi.

(v: Comfort zone, Long-haul travel, Safety)

~

ADVICE *(giving and receiving)*

If somebody asks for your advice, give it thoughtfully and gracefully in the knowledge that they will, of course, ignore it. Ditto if you are asking for advice. Receive it thoughtfully and graciously before you ignore it. If you are on the receiving end of unasked-for advice, just ignore it. However, a father's advice to his daughter on her twenty-first birthday – 'However much you have to drink you must remember what you said and did in the morning. Never interfere in a great love affair and don't sleep with your secretary' – has stood her in good stead.

(v: Affairs, Insomnia, I don't)

~

AFFAIRS

Should you or shouldn't you? The answer is that you shouldn't. But, as it is crucial to the excitement of having an affair to let all experience, wisdom and proffered advice go out of the window, you are probably going to go ahead anyway.

An affair can be thrilling: excitingly illicit, deeply passionate and often liberating on many levels – all the things that a long-term relationship isn't. However, affairs can also bring heartbreak, not just to the two people involved, but also to their respective partners, children and extended families.

If you are unable to practice self-restraint here are some guidelines:

1. Don't have an affair with your husband's best friend.

2. Be discreet.

3. Garters and stockings are always good.

4. Don't neglect your children.

5. Remember your friends, you may need them in due course.

6. However wonderful it is, remind yourself occasionally that most affairs have a lifetime of six months to two years.

7. Don't slag off your lover's partner, or join in when he does it. It's unfair and it's undignified.

8. If your lover is in a relationship and you are single, only you are allowed to set the rules.

9. If your lover tells you he wants to try and make his marriage work, have the good grace to let him try.

10. Occasionally put yourself through the shipwreck scenario, i.e. what are all the long-term options, both good and bad. Be honest with yourself.

11. If your lover's partner becomes seriously ill in any way, his job is to support her. You must put your relationship on hold.

12. Protect your heart.

> *(v: Camiknickers, Contraception, Creative corsetry, Family therapy, Grief, I don't, Lawyers, Loss, Money matters, Rejection, Teenagers)*

⤲

AGE

'Age is enlightenment at gunpoint.'
– ANNA HALPIN

'No woman should ever be quite accurate about her age.
It looks so calculating.'
– OSCAR WILDE

'Age cannot wither her, nor custom stale
her infinite variety.'
– *ANTONY AND CLEOPATRA*, II. II., WILLIAM SHAKESPEARE

'Aging is the result of an accumulation of
random molecular damage.'
– LEWIS WOLPERT

⤲

AGELESS FASHION

'Fashion fades, only style remains the same.'
– COCO CHANEL

It's called style. Some people have it and some people just don't.

ৼ

(THE) AGE OF BEREAVEMENT

There is a moment in life when you find that you are attending more divorces and funerals than you are weddings and christenings. Losing a close friend or mentor or partner is acutely painful and with the death of both parents comes the final realization that there is no road back. This milestone is complicated to deal with and you may feel alienated from your partner and/or children. After all, you are meant to be a grown-up, aren't you? It might be worth seeking professional help. Or talk to your friends. Many of your friends will be going through or have already gone through similar experiences. Allow yourself to mourn properly, focus on the good times. On bad days it really is important to use the coping tools of the mundane to get you through, i.e. airing the bedroom, making a fire, planting some geraniums in pots. It is also helpful to 'be the poet of your own life'. Keep a diary, write poetry, write letters. If you find it hard to concentrate, watch TV, listen to music and/ or the radio. Sleep. See your mates. Remember that the darkest hour is before the dawn. Hope is essential. You will get through.

(v: BFF, Mentors, Therapy)

ം

AGONY

*'One often learns more from ten days of agony
than ten years of contentment.'*
– MERLE SHAIN [JOURNALIST AND WRITER]

Emotional agony, it's unmistakable and it can have physical symptoms such as lack of hunger, swift weight loss and feelings of acute stress, which are often accompanied by a racing, churning manic behavior. We can take medication to overcome it. Or we may choose to live with emotional agony at least for a limited period of time. Therapists will argue that this acute pain, arising as it usually does out of separation from a loved one, through divorce or death, is a spiritual event that marks a moment of transformation. It is a journey into the underworld. The message from the gods is that if we can go through the fire we will find greater self-acceptance, self-knowledge and understanding as a result and return to the land of the living intact.

(v: Age of bereavement, Persephone)

ം

A GOOD MAN IS HARD TO FIND
But not impossible.

(v: Good husband material, Hope, Little black book, Top table)

ALCOHOL

'Who loves not wine, woman, and song
Remains a fool his whole life long.'

– ATTRIBUTED TO MARTIN LUTHER

(v: Bad habits, Booze, Champagne, Cocktails, Codependency,
Dipsomania, Drunk-dialing, Grappa, Insomnia)

ALL ABOUT EVE

'She, as a veil, down to a slender waist
Her unadorned golden tresses wore
Dishevelled. but in wanton ringlets waved
As the vine curls her tendrils, which implied subjection, but
required with gentle sway.
And by her, yielded, by him best received
Yielded with coy submission, modest pride, And sweet, reluctant,
amorous delay.'

– *PARADISE LOST*, BOOK IV, JOHN MILTON

~

ALLERGIES

For some reason it's hard to be sympathetic if somebody tells you that they can't eat Brazil nuts, nevertheless the fashion for allergies underlies a real twenty-first-century problem. We are too clean, our houses are too clean. And because of the current 'expert advice' on breastfeeding and weaning, our babies may not be getting a wide enough variety of foodstuffs and accompanying bacteria at a young enough age. Couple this with the extraordinarily successful worldwide campaign to eradicate killer diseases and the result is that we are developing incomplete immune systems in bodies that no longer have to fight external intruders (viral and bacterial) and are succumbing to a range of autoimmune diseases instead. It's tiresome but we need to be responsible and sympathetic to those who suffer from allergies and meet their dietary requirements without a murmur. If you suspect that you may be allergic to something, we won't call you a moaning minny, just please go and get tested. The upside of all of this, for the less house-proud among us, is that there is a valid reason for not cleaning the kitchen floor more than once a week.

(v: Meds)

ᘒ

ALLURE

The essence of allure is to be in a private relationship with oneself. Allure is an ageless quality that combines sexuality with ancient wisdom, secret confidence, inner depth and the ability to remain still in a busy room. Contemporary ideas of beauty and the overexposure of models and actresses in newspapers and magazines means that it is rare to see a famous person who looks alluring. There are just too many lightbulbs flashing in the background. The woman in the street, on the other hand, has every chance to develop these qualities.

(v: Elegance, Maturity, Secret confidence, Style)

ᘒ

(THE) ALMOST DATE
(AND HOW TO AVOID IT THE SECOND TIME AROUND)

There was a time when if a man asked you out, you knew what his intentions were. But twenty-first-century dating is a minefield. Is he asking you out – or just out?

In the past, love was a formal contract. Today, romance is so laidback it's horizontal. Sometimes being laissez-faire can suit. It can give you time to get to know him without feeling pressured or rushed. However, if you are already very keen on him and/or very much in the dating zone or just somebody who likes knowing where they stand, here's a checklist from the writers of *He's Just Not That Into You*:

1. Expect a public excursion, a meal and some hand-holding.

2. Hopefully a message post-date to say he had a nice time.

3. Then some kind of further contact within three days.

Hanging out is not dating. If in doubt of his intentions, ask another man. As women, in our desire to be kind and supportive, we often do more harm than good by perpetuating our friends' mad romantic fantasies, i.e. checking out wedding dresses in shops or thinking up baby names, but there are times when we need tough love from the Dating Nazis and in turn your friends might need it from you too.

A trusted male friend will give it to you straight – and shoot down all the sexcuses. Exhibit A: there is no such thing as mixed messages. If he's not calling you, you're not on his mind. Exhibit B: The dreaded 'It's not you, it's me' is a clue to run for the hills. Men are not complicated. If they like you, they phone.

(v: Pep talk from a fiery redhead)

~

ALONENESS (AS OPPOSED TO LONELINESS)
'I've just done what I damn well wanted to, and I've made enough money to support myself, and ain't afraid of being alone.'
– KATHARINE HEPBURN

'The freedom of our age is that you can be alone.
The price is that you might also have to feel lonely.'
– ALAIN DE BOTTON [PHILOSOPHER]

'Never less lonely than when completely alone.'
– CICERO

When you are busy, you aren't alone. Loneliness doesn't sit well with the upbeat image that we like to project to the outside world. People will admit to being depressed (intriguing and melancholy) or drinking too much (spontaneous and fun-loving), but we won't admit to being lonely because it makes us feel a failure.

In modern times there is ever increasing pressure for women to appear to be 'self-contained'. Any kind of neediness is frowned upon but the truth is that loneliness can have a profound effect on our lives. Recent research has shown that it can damage the chemical and electrical responses in our immune systems that help prevent illness. Some studies argue that loneliness is a bigger killer than cancer or heart disease.

Our monkey ancestors lived in social groups and we have evolved into sociable human beings. The word 'lonely' wasn't used in the contemporary sense until the eighteenth century, partly because everyone lived so closely together that there was never a chance to be so. The Romantic poets changed the concept of loneliness with vivid intensity. Wordsworth's 'I Wandered Lonely as a Cloud', expresses a new tension between the individual self and society.

If you are feeling lonely the first task is to identify whether this is something to be 'cured', or something that needs to be 'managed'? It is also important to distinguish between aloneness, i.e. learning to enjoy a period of solitude whether it is chosen or enforced, and the real, grinding loneliness that can make you feel like hell. Most important of all, don't beat yourself up for feeling lonely.

(v: Flow, Keep your diary full)

ભભ

ALPHA FEMALES
(v: Ambition, Top girls)

ભભ

AMBITION

Why is this still such a dirty word for women? For men ambition is a necessary and desirable part of their lives, but women so often play down their achievements for fear of being seen as egotistic or selfish – or worse still, a 'bitch'. Surely we all want our efforts and accomplishments acknowledged? It's perfectly acceptable to engage in competition. Ambition gets us up in the morning and it motivates us to keep going when things get rough. So why the double standard? When a male boss is cross at work we excuse him because he's a perfectionist. When a woman demands high standards, she's having a hissy fit. Remember, ambition is neutral: it's how you use it that defines whether you're operating in a healthy or an unhealthy way.

(v: Alpha females)

ललल

AMBIVALENCE (TO A LOVER)

Ambivalence about a lover usually signifies that there are big emotions at play, either positive or negative or both. If you are experiencing ambivalence about a partner, or aspects of your relationship, you need to get to the heart of the matter and be truthful about your feelings, pronto!

(v: Bachelors, Rejection)

ललल

AMBIVALENCE (TO AN EX-LOVER)

The ultimate revenge for someone who has broken your heart.

(v: Rejection)

ललल

AMORALITY

We may argue that we live in an amoral age but every individual should have principles.

(v: Bachelors, Personal code of conduct)

ललल

ANAL SEX

Beloved of ex-English public school boys, particularly Old Etonians, some women find they can work this into their repertoire. It's also an ancient, though not fail-safe, method of contraception. If it's not your cup of tea, don't get too worked up about it. Simply apply the once in three rule and if you still don't like it you are allowed to say 'no'.

❧

ANGELOU, MAYA [ICON]

'I've learned that people will forget what you said, people will forget what you did, but people will never forget how you made them feel.'

❧

ANGER

'I was angry with my friend:
I told my wrath, my wrath did end.
I was angry with my foe:
I told it not, my wrath did grow.'
– 'A POISON TREE', WILLIAM BLAKE

We could all benefit from cultivating an authentic voice for ourselves. We need to learn to express real feelings at work, with friends, in love, toward our children.

Of course, getting explosive in a situation isn't impressive. Rage has a childlike quality about it, so, while in the short term you may have a feeling of release, in the medium to long term nobody respects you for it.

No one wants to bottle resentment up. People become confused by your passivity and lose respect for you, cf. Lady Bertram in *Mansfield Park*. Dates slip through your hands and lazier friends take advantage.

Assertiveness is about recognizing that you are entitled to certain things. So be confident in expressing your feelings or views while respecting that other people have them too. Get it right, and you'll be able to pole-vault over the whole anger thing altogether, while getting a little more of your own way some of the time, which, after all, is only fair but don't forget that righteous anger, if justified, can be extremely liberating too.

(v: Boxing)

ANIMAL PRINTS

The rules are: leopard skin for fat days; zebra for bags, belts and shoes; snakeskin for cuffs and collars . . . We could write a sonnet to the sheer joy that is the animal print. Never out of fashion probably because they're never strictly in, animal prints always look chic even when they're retro.

No doubt our fascination is rooted in our primitive selves. We may atavistically associate animal prints with animal characteristics. In African tribal societies, the skin of a lion is worn to imbue a warrior with that particular animal's fabled characteristics.

There are sartorial rules, of course, especially if you don't want to look like a mini-me Rod Stewart. Keep it to one key piece (coat, shoes or scarf). Remember the only color that really works with animal prints is black, although we would very occasionally make an exception for leopard skin with a splash of red or pink.

And these days – unless you live in Outer Siberia – there is absolutely no excuse for buying the real thing. The new fakes are so fabulous they scream haute couture.

(v: Scarfology)

༖

ANNOYING WOMEN WHO LIKE FOOTBALL

There is an ever-increasing trend in women who pretend to like football in an effort to bond with their 'man'. This involves donning football jerseys, going to football games and drinking pints down at the pub. It's irritating because it feels so forced. Eventually these women stop having to pretend to like football and actually do like football. This smacks of Pavlov's dog.

༖

APOLOGIZING

If you have behaved badly you need to apologize. Whether you have been irritable to somebody at work, overreacted to something a friend or partner has said, or shouted at your children just for the sake of it, however hard it feels and however resentful you feel about doing it (because of course it's always nicer to be right), you should make amends. They will feel better. You will feel better and although this may seem counterintuitive, because some people will only respond to iron will, cf. Barack Obama/Osama bin Laden, surely, ultimately people will love and respect you for doing it. It is particularly important that your children learn from you in this regard. Everybody has arguments, it's your ability to make a good peace that marks you out as a functioning person.

(v: Family therapy, It seemed like a good idea at the time)

ARMS

The punctuation marks of our body: to hug, to hold, to stop, to seize, to embrace. The arms can be all things to all people and we express ourselves constantly through a huge variety of movements. They show excitement, fear and love. They carry and work for us. They hold food and our babies, and are, very often, strangely ignored. A beautiful, well-toned arm is very sexy, and light work with weights and regular swimming will deliver results. However, if you do have a tendency of bingo wings, a forgiving cropped sleeve will do the trick.

To say nothing, of course, of the elegant and serene *port de bras* in ballet, meaning literally 'the carriage of the arms', where the aim is to be graceful, poised and seamless at all times. Love your arms.

(v: Boxing, Frocks, Pilates)

(An) Arrangement

Who'd have known it? The arrangement is back in vogue. Does it mean many marriages that have hit the rocks could have trolleyed on if there had been a French-style/1940's 'arrangement' in place?

The definition of an arrangement is having a guy dangling around and then meeting him every few weeks for an elegant dinner or some seriously good sex (occasionally both). Think more Graham Greene than F. Scott Fitzgerald.

So, an arrangement means not getting hot under the collar, hysterically needy or sad. You are both just enjoying each other's company and having a good time. It's grown-up, very cool and you don't gossip about it or get demanding. It just is. Plus, it can continue for ages because there is no melodrama attached – that's a double plus.

(v: Affairs, Camiknickers, Cinq à sept)

(The) Art of makeup

Less is more where makeup is concerned, and it's great skin that counts. That said, a good concealer popped on the inner corner of the eyes and around the reddish area of the nose is an excellent idea. Eyeliner inside the lashes defines the eye, as does a cat flick on the outside edge of the eye.

Lipstick – many wouldn't leave home without it. Keep key items of makeup in your handbag at all times and reapply.

Foundation is good for parties where, if you're lucky, you might find yourself getting a bit hot and bothered.

(v: False eyelashes, Lipstick)

⊱

ASTROLOGY

Astrology . . . a tricky one this. Especially, if like us, you love reading astrologers in newspapers and magazines, but wonder, quite simply, do they just rehash the same stuff, e.g. is Taurus interchangeable with Scorpio?

Of course, planetary action is always appealing, particularly when the likes of *Dr. Who* are involved, and it naturally feels even more plausible if your astrological reading is super-positive. But, does it really help in the long run?

Perhaps closer to the truth is that we are all looking for a little bit of hope and positivity in our lives. So if you read for the forty-seventh time that 'today you might attend a party or group event with some friends', we suggest you look into the following alternatives instead:

(v: Chocolate, Comfort zone, Soothsayers)

༚

AT FIRST I WAS AFRAID, I WAS PETRIFIED

If you suspect a obsessive-compulsive anxiety disorder (OCD) in yourself, or other people, you need to know that its main feature is that masses of time are spent on useless and futile tasks, i.e. washing your hands, checking that the oven is off or that the door is properly locked, in the vain and probably unconscious hope that these actions will help diminish worry or distress. They do not and they will not and, of course, the endless participation in repetitive and excessive anxieties begins to compound the problem because you are too busy cleaning the bathroom to face up to the reasons why you are anxious in the first place. If you are displaying any of these symptoms get help as soon as possible.

(v: Allergies)

༚

ATHILL, DIANA [ICON]

'I'd been in love and thought I was going to end up happily married with children – a very simple wish, but I'd failed to make it and that was more spirit weakening than I realized. When I got rid of it in my early forties by writing it out, it was like a new life. I felt like a new person and I've felt like that ever since.'

AUNTS

Nowadays as the result of the extended family and the close ties between female friends (sometimes closer than those between sisters), anybody can be an 'aunt'. Aunts as evoked by P. G. Wodehouse and Roald Dahl are hopefully a thing of the past. Whether you are blood related or not, an aunt can have a special status in a woman's life. An aunt's role is necessarily fluid. From a mother's point of view, an aunt is probably a friend whom she can entirely trust, who shares her values and will take over, temporarily, if she needs help with childcare or the going gets tough. From a child's perspective, an aunt is somebody who is really good fun for adventures and treats and mini-breaks to Euro Disney. For an aunt, it is fun to be part of a family but not have to be there every day.

(v: Babies, Childfree, Godmothers, Teenagers)

BABIES (YOUR OWN OR OTHER PEOPLE'S)
"Every child begins the world again."
– *WALDEN*, HENRY DAVID THOREAU

"Father asked us what was God's noblest work. Anna said men,
but I said babies. Men are often bad, but babies never are."
– *Louisa May Alcott*

Babies are some of the most joyous and life-enhancing people you'll ever get to meet. If you haven't got one of your own try and make sure that you spend proper time with other people's. If you are a new godmother make the most of that connection – if an exhausted friend needs help, support and babysitting, offer! Babies may not be able to speak but they recognize familiar faces and babies and young children remember somebody who takes a genuine interest in them.

ℰ⌒

BABY DYKES

'Girls who are boys, who like boys to be girls, who do boys like they're girls, who do girls like they're boys.' Fashion has celebrated dyke chic, with boots and biker jackets, scrubbed faces and urchin crops. Certainly the new generation of early twenty-somethings no longer need to define themselves as straight or gay, and it's perfectly acceptable not only to be unsure, but to be neither. Diehard card-carrying feminists with dangly earrings may worry about the lack of sexual politics – but frankly it's a hell of a lot better than our teenage years when to be called a 'lesbo' in the school corridor induced a hot blush of shame.

One fine day how you dress will say nothing about who you take to bed (hurrah). And frankly no one will care, but in the meantime increasing sexual choice for women empowers everybody.

(v: Lesbian bed death)

ℰ⌒

BACHELORS (COMMITTED, TOXIC OR OTHERWISE)

Rather like 'war' what are they actually good for? The answer is that they have many uses but you must promise one thing, don't for even one nanosecond fantasize, contemplate or think that they will break the habit of a lifetime and fall in love with you and want to marry you. You have been warned. Now to practical matters: it is very helpful to have a few bachelors in your little black book; they specialize in being charming and fun at dinner parties; they may, if it suits them (selfishness is a ubiquitous quality among this particular demographic), agree to escort you to a frightening social event; sometimes they can be a friend with benefits and that's good for your health if nothing else, and presumably because they don't have children of their own (or none they'll admit to), they are often extraordinarily sweet with other people's. This can occasionally begin to melt your heart but don't let it. Long-term bachelors can become very good friends indeed, but be realistic and be compassionate too, it may look as if they are having a lot of carefree fun but they are plowing a lonely furrow.

(v: Boundaries, Complete wankers, Little black book, Narcissus)

~

BAD BOYS

'I want guitar heroes and boys who were raised on the streets by wolves. Atilla the Hun is my basic dream lover.'
– STORY OF MY LIFE, JAY MCINERNEY

(v: Caveman moment)

~

BAD HABITS

It's easy to spot other people's and very hard to own up to your own. Some bad habits are simply revolting, e.g. picking scabs off your legs or cutting your toenails in public places, and you will be judged accordingly. Others, such as interrupting other people while they are talking, are commonplace and they can really piss people off. Weirdly, the bad habits that you find in others are sometimes the bad habits you can't see in yourself and it may take a friend or lover to point them out to you. Accept their comments gracefully.

(v: Affairs, Cocktails, Dipsomania)

෩

BALLOONING WEIGHT

For health reasons, among many others, nip it in the bud while you can.

(v: Boxing, Carbohydrates, Climacteric, Comfort zone, Diets, Eat your greens, Trampolining, Waist)

෩

BANANA

The handbag essential. An instant energy boost, and rich in tryptophan – one of the twenty common amino acids that make up all proteins – which the body converts into serotonin, known to make you more relaxed and happy. And can we just applaud the brilliant no-waste packaging?

(v: Eat your greens, Fruit)

✍

BEAUTY

*'I go to bed early. I meditate. I eat all the correct foods.
I don't smoke or drink, and I believe with a passion in myself. You
can only beat nature when you show the bitch who's boss.'*

– MAE WEST

It is said that before the age of 40 you have the face that God
gives you and after 40 the face that you deserve. What is clear
is that no amount of money or surgery can give you that inner
glow that comes with the combination of self-acceptance,
secret confidence and a general connection to the national grid
of love and happiness. A dash of quiet spirituality doesn't go
amiss either.

*(v: Beauty industry, Bien dans ta peau, Eat your greens,
Facial acupuncture, Secret confidence)*

✍

(THE) BEAUTY INDUSTRY

The global cosmetics, toiletries and fragrance industry is worth
$9 billion and an average woman might spend $200,000 on
beauty products in her lifetime.

Anti-aging is the holy grail of the beauty industry. It is the
promise in the pot, the elixir of youth where the 'appearance
of fine lines may diminish', albeit temporarily and with them
a great deal of cash. Often the domain of psychobabble and
pseudoscience, it's a question of sorting the wheat from the

chaff. Moisturizing, massaging, exercising your face and controlling lymphatic drainage are key. Much of the beauty industry, ironically, is antiwomen in that it trades on insecurities and low self-esteem.

Make sure your face is your fortune and not theirs.

(v: Facial acupuncture, Facial exercises)

⁓

BEDS

You want the best bed you can afford, the larger the better, especially if you've got kids. Preferably one with a mattress cobbled together by fairies with extra fluff and some stardust sprinkled on top, though do watch out for the odd, strategically placed pea. However, if you are partner- or child-free you can just make the most of your bed and spread out – you should sleep beautifully.

Ideally, beds should have fresh sheets weekly and be aired daily. We also really like the rather retro 'bolster', which is great for reading in bed. If cash is tight there are plenty of cheap options. Trawl the small ads for secondhand beds, although buy a new mattress to avoid bedbugs. You can paint a wooden frame and create amazing valances with vintage fabric, or chintzy old curtains. Garage sales are usually piled high with cheap sheets, pillowcases and old curtains. It simply doesn't matter if it's not all 'matchy matchy'. The featherbed is possibly the most scrumptious (and relatively new) bed accessory on the market. It is a great fat ploofy layer of fluff that you fold over the mattress before putting the sheets on. All very dreamy and comfy and bouncy. So much so that you may decide to stay in bed all day, and who could blame you?

(v: Insomnia)

ぐ⌒

BEING BORING
We're against it.

(v: Bores)

ぐ⌒

BENDERS

Sometimes in life you just have to let go. Going on a bender is traditionally seen as a male preserve but increasingly women are doing it too. Sometimes benders creep up on one. You know, the promise of a quick drink with a friend at the end of work turns into a big night out, or a Friday night out with mates turns into a very long, alcohol-fueled weekend (occasionally culminating in eating tripe, shoeless, in a workman's café at 5 a.m. on a Monday morning).

A great bender is a holiday from real life: a spontaneous way of marking the end of a relationship, a divorce or to celebrate a landmark birthday. It's often a rite of passage for friends, male and female, confidences are exchanged, relationships consolidated and the unspoken rule is, as a mark of your deepening respect and love for one another, that whatever your various states of disrepair nobody's going to remind you of your extravagant pole dancing in a downtown dive bar. Or maybe just a little bit . . .

In fact, a key feature of a bender is that you probably won't remember anything when you wake up, you may well have lost a number of your belongings and you may end up in a hotel room, though not necessarily the one that you had booked for yourself the previous evening. However, fragments of memory will begin to return during the course of the morning and you will probably find yourself looking into the mouth of hell. You may discover that drunk-dialing and a toxic bachelor or two have entered the mix, which is the point where regret, self-doubt and paranoia begin to creep in. The two solutions are either to butch it out at work or go to bed. Relief will finally come at about 7 p.m. when the miasma begins to lift. You can, of course, attempt to guard against all these things – eat carbohydrates before you go out; drink a glass of water after every glass of champagne; appoint a drink monitor; only take one credit card with you, and so on and so forth – but look into your heart and ask yourself truthfully and honestly whether such an evening really counts as a bender?

(v: Alcohol, Booty calls, Booze, Breaking the rules,
Cocktails, Dipsomania, Drunk-dialing, It seemed like a good idea
at the time, Make the most of it, Regrets)

ᴜᴟᴧ

BEREAVEMENT
'Where grief is fresh, any attempt to divert it only irritates.'
– SAMUEL JOHNSON

'This is not the time to repress your feelings.
Allow yourself to go mad as you like.'
– NICHOLAS ARDIZZONE
(v: Age of grief, Counseling, Grief, Loss, Therapy)

ᴜᴟᴧ

BE WARM
Happy people aren't especially lucky or beautiful but they connect well to others and as a result they tend to have rich personal relationships. In adolescence we assume nihilism is cool. But as you get older, warmth becomes a seriously hot property. Stop worrying whether people will find you weird and intense. Other people are generally nicer than you think. And if they're not? Your goodwill combined with good behavior is the best form of body armor.

If you insist on maintaining your ice-cold *froideur* you will eventually become an empty fridge. If you reach an understanding that it doesn't matter what people think about you then you have become entirely free.

(v: Secret confidence)

෮෪

BE WELL INFORMED

There is no excuse not to be. The radio, newspapers, websites or well-chosen periodicals, such as *Newsweek*, will keep you up to date. It's important to take a view on politics but remember to change the subject if it looks as though your radical views on Sarah Palin, global warming and politics look set to ruin somebody else's beautifully organized dinner party.

(v: Good stuff that's free, Libraries, the Queen)

෮෪

(THE) BFF

'A friend is, as it were, a second self.'

– CICERO

Your BFF, usually but not always, is the closest thing you have to family without being family: she is the person you can be most honest to; she is utterly trustworthy; never judgmental, she is the keeper of your innermost dreams and desires. Although she may from time to time point you in the right direction and administer a necessary pep talk, she is also the best of fun and you can literally spend days at a time talking on the phone or chatting on the beach. If you don't spend enough time with your BFF, because of the demands of family and work, you will miss her enormously but once you are together again it's as though she has never been away. It is also the mark of a BFF that she never really makes demands. If this sounds too idyllic, prepare for the occasional twinge of irritation, that's a reality, but also recognize that you quite simply can't imagine life without her and celebrate that fact.

(v: Catching the bouquet, Pep talk from a fiery redhead)

~

BIEN DANS TA PEAU

This charming French expression is true, elegant and simply means 'to feel happy in one's skin'. If you are *bien dans ta peau*, you are not self-conscious, or mirror grabbing or in need of constant flattery.

(v: Flow)

~

BIG BABIES

'Oh give me a break' is the battle cry of those who have the onerous task of having to deal with a 'big baby' on a regular basis. This could be your lover, your darling child, your BFF or a colleague at work. Big babyism has no regard for age or gender. Warning signs are that they moan constantly. The big baby (and this is the really irritating bit) makes an absolute meal of helping anybody else out, to the point where they become no help at all and quite simply you wish you hadn't asked them in the first place. A big baby is also perennially moody and basically just way too delicate for modern life. Have we striven so hard to free ourselves from the shackles of a patriarchal society to have to put up with such nonsense? The answer is NO. The solution is

DON'T DO IT. So to all you BBs out there, 'Spare us the labor pains and, quite frankly, grow up!'

ᏋᏟᕉ

BIRTHDAYS

They come and they go, and they come again. Taking a fluid attitude to your own is probably the best idea, as life changes, and with it your ideals.

(v: Little bit of what you fancy does you good)

ᏋᏟᕉ

BITCHES AND HOS

For heaven's sake! Where has this ridiculous kind of chat come from? The pointy finger turns toward rap music, but loads of men and, sad to say, a few women – whatever their economic circumstances or the color of their skin – have jumped on this pernicious bandwagon. Stop it now!

(v: Caveman moment)

ᏋᏟᕉ

BLAIZE, IMMODESTY

(v: Confidence, Role models)

∾

BLAME

Blame becomes increasingly ugly as one gets older, and there is something rather forlorn about a grown woman still blaming her parents. Either park it in the long-term car park and throw away the keys or, if you still feel weighed down by burning resentments stemming from childhood experiences, the time has to come to take responsibility for them yourself and go to see a therapist. Long-term grievances should not be allowed to fester. Also, it is surely, unless grotesque abuse has taken place, the place of the grown-up child to smooth the path for aging parents. Olive branches can grow anywhere, especially with global warming. Start cultivating your olive grove now. The ability to forgive is one of the greatest of all human qualities.

(v: Big babies)

∾

BLOGGING

Gives you a voice and a presence in a very noisy world. From Julie Powell who cooked all of Julia Child's recipes (immortalized in the film, *Julie & Julia)* to sexpert Belle de Jour, a micro-blog can become a global hit. You may even get paid-for advertising. But remember the male blogosphere can be bruising. Ignore the trolls!

∾

Bloom

'The day came when the wish to remain tight in a
bud was more painful than the risk it took to blossom.'

– Anaïs Nin

(v: Rain)

∾

Blow-dries

A blow-dry is not a replacement for a good haircut but it can lift morale faster than a large glass of wine. It's a good idea to have several salons on speed dial for a last-minute appointment. And shop around. A blow-dry can cost anything from $20–$80 but think ahead, it may not be worth paying a small fortune for a senior stylist if you're going to go swimming tomorrow.

(v: Necessary vanity, Secret confidence)

∾

Blow jobs

'Do as you would be done by' is our motto here. It's also terribly good for the cheek muscles, ladies, and some people claim that it can trigger the start of labor. Do keep it up!

(v: Childbirth)

∽

BLUEBERRIES

1. Possibly the ultimate super-food. Many nutritionists believe that if you make only one change to your diet, add blueberries. Bake them in muffins, snack on them at your desk to beat sugar cravings . . . Keep a bag in the freezer, so you always have some on hand.

2. Just 100g (4oz) of blueberries contains the same amount of age-defying antioxidants as five servings of most other fruit and vegetables. To remind you: antioxidants help guard against a range of cancers, heart disease, asthma and age-related neurological diseases. They do this by preventing infectious bacteria from clinging to the wall of the gut, bladder and urethra. Blueberries also offer protection against cystitis.

3. High in vitamin C and a good source of fiber, blueberries contain a compound, pterostilbene, which acts to protect the heart in the same way as cholesterol-lowering drugs. They also contain anthocyanins, which give blueberries their blue color.

4. Blueberries contain polyphenols, which combat the effects of free radicals, a key cause of wrinkles, so they keep skin looking younger for longer. They also help the body to make collagen, which keeps skin supple.

5. It's good to eat lots of red or blue plants (watermelon, cranberries, bilberries, grapes, prunes) that contain anthocyanins – many new cutting-edge beauty products contain them because of their cell-protective powers.

6. While we are on the subject, look out for makeup containing an ingredient called Purpulyn, which has anti-aging benefits. It is found in blueberries and also in plants such as dark tulips and black orchids.

   (v: Banana, Detox, Eat your greens, Super-foods)

⸎

BLUES

The blues have a special quality that is different from depression, grief or all around low spirits. They are characterized by weepiness, flashes of intense sadness and the feeling that one is secretly unable to cope. They can be triggered by a variety of things, both small and large: remembrance of things past; the passing of the seasons; a dear friend moving to live abroad; sheer tiredness; the intense hormonal changes that can come with the birth of a baby; the prospect of a family event; but whatever the trigger it is worth taking them a little bit seriously. Vitamins, exercise, a good night's sleep, cutting out alcohol for a bit, a brilliant and engrossing book, the companionship of old friends can all help to combat the blues. From a creative point of view, happiness writes white, while some of the best poems and songs in history have been inspired by a good dose of the blues.

(v: Babies, Depression, Winter)

⸎

BLUESTOCKING

Is the term given to women of an academic bent who, in theory, will never compromise their intellectual standards. If this sounds too severe the name implies an undercurrent of something more vibrant and more sexual. History tells us that the bluestocking emblem dates back to 1400 Venice where erudite men and women of the moment met at the society Compagnie della Calza to discuss culture and politics. However, it was not until 1750 that an upper-class, London-based cultural milieu founded a similar society. This was greeted with delight from some, and a fair amount of derision from one or two disgruntled husbands. But the society and then the term "bluestocking" stuck. In an age where the modern media tells us that it is impossible to be both pretty and clever (if you are, you will be punished accordingly) do remind yourself to wear your bluestockings with pride.

BOBBY PIN

When you're feeling at your most dreary, never underestimate the transformative power of the bobby pin. It can make you look and feel ten years younger and its slightly retro style makes it perfect if you are wearing vintage.

(v: Vintage)

BODY MANAGEMENT

'Many young girls are constantly consumed by controlling and managing their body image to the extent that they are much more involved in the production of the self than in living.'

– SUSIE ORBACH

BOLT-HOLE

This might be a palace, a wattle-daubed cottage, a teeny beach hut on a windswept shore, a spare bedroom or even a garden shed, but it's your kingdom and yours alone, where you can grab a bit of peace and quiet and gather your thoughts. Or not. Sometimes just a little light gazing out of the window does the trick. Women, in-between work and home, are not granted much personal space, so your only option may be to grant it to yourself. If you are of an arts and crafts bent, have fun doing up your bolt-hole and making it your own. It's somewhere

where you can finish that book, write poetry, or simply read the newspaper. Somewhere where you can just 'take five'.

(v: Beach huts, Embroidery, Going to Prison,
Infinite vistas, Poetry, Studio)

BOMBSHELLS

Pulled up, pushed in, and generally shaken all about, the Bombshell is a name given to a drop-dead gorgeous siren. Marilyn Monroe in *Some Like It Hot* is the benchmark. It is also the name for the ubiquitous cocktail dress, which can cover an absolute multitude of sins and dress you up like a knickerbocker glory. You need nothing more than a cardigan and a pair of pumps to go with it and you're away. With ruched paneling and a sort of superstructure that would have made newspaper magnate Howard Hughes, who among other things designed the ultimate bra for Jane Russell, green with envy, every Dangerous Woman about town needs at least one or even two of these babies in her wardrobe.

(v: Body management, Frocks)

∾

BONES

Plenty of sunshine, lots of exercise, as well as calcium in the form of milk, eggs, cheese, yogurt, oily fish, sardines, salmon, tuna, spinach.

(v: Exercise, Knees)

∾

BOOBS

Voluptuous curves are back. And people really do love a proper bosom. It's one of life's pleasures. Women probably spend even more time admiring them than men.

Of course, it helps that the current rise of tailored shifts, corsets and stockings are so flattering to curvy birds, and it's wonderful that the days of *La Dolce Vita*, when women were supposed to have milky white globes spilling over their dresses are, gloriously, back. The French have a lovely phrase for it too: '*Elle a tout le monde dans le balcon*' (she has everyone in the balcony). But how does one dress the breasts? Or rather, how low should you go?

It's so easy to make a sartorial faux pas with cleavage. Party frocks with a daring neckline can look very good on the hanger, but get it wrong and everything goes into freefall. You need to understand structure. The perfect breasts are pert not pendulous. So think in 3D, and sort out the bras, and/or the corsets to go with each frock. Too much cleavage can make the difference between being perceived as a gorgeously sexual human being and a cartoon slapper. For those of us over the age of 35 there are clear rules for exposing skin. Make sure you're well supported, avoid slashed to the waist affairs (tit tape doesn't work), never wear a crossover neckline (you get that awful crêpey crease), and don't expose too much leg if breasts are on show.

But not everyone has to do boobs. If you are a flat chester, enjoy revealing toned shoulders – the new erogenous zone, cf. the Duchess of Cambridge and Michelle Obama.

(v: Bras, Creative corsetry, Curves)

やん

BOOTY CALLS

You may or may not have been on the receiving end of a booty call but it works like this. It's about 10 p.m. You are planning to have an early night when your phone goes. It's a bloke who you have met once or twice, you may even have slept with him. He is sitting in the pub with some friends and he is a little bit drunk. The conversation is genial but the meaning is clear, he wants to have sex. So far so good but the tricky part of all of this is, do you? If you are confident and ready to throw caution to the wind, put on a pair of clean knickers, jump into a cab and make the connection, or is it going to be a firm 'no' and a cup of hot milk and early bed? It's a difficult one and much depends on how you are feeling about yourself. If the answer is confident and sexy and up for anything, then go for it while taking the necessary precautions. However, if you are feeling in any way miserable, vulnerable or lonely, turn your phone off, put on your fluffy slippers and reach for your battered copy of *Gone with the Wind*.

The good news is that our survey shows that if you want to make a booty call yourself you will have a 99.9% success rate. It's great to know that in the battle of the sexes women sometimes have the upper hand.

(v: Alcohol, Drunk-dialing, It seemed like a good idea at the time, Mercy fuck, Regrets)

BOOZE

(v: Alcohol, Ballooning weight, Booty calls, Champagne, Cocktails, Diets, Dipsomania, Drunk-dialing, Grappa, Martini, Quests)

BOREDOM

'. . . *that state of suspended animation in which things are started and nothing begins, the mood of diffuse restlessness, which contains that most absurd and paradoxical wish, the wish for a desire.*'

– ADAM PHILLIPS

BORES

'*Blessed is the man who, having nothing to say, abstains from giving us wordy evidence of the fact.*'

– GEORGE ELIOT

'Only dull people are brilliant at breakfast.'
– OSCAR WILDE

We all know one or two bores and if you are becoming one yourself we suggest you snap out of it sharpish, although, of course, a key characteristic of being a bore is that you don't know you are one.

An atypical bore is somebody who collars you at a jam, and then does something unutterably rude, such as grill you about what A levels you took when you are trying to laugh and drink a martini. A bore is somebody who doesn't realize that a party is for amusing chitchat, and that it is everybody's duty to be a little bit up and light and amusing. If in trouble with a bore, courtesy dictates that you talk to them for a long five minutes but then you can make your excuses pronto and dart off to the loo, or pretend that you have to go outside and make a call. Chances are there will be smokers out there and they are usually much more fun.

(v: Guests, Walking away)

BOTOX

To Botox or not to Botox, that is the question. Most women spend 90% of the time saying they wouldn't have Botox and then when they meet somebody who has had it done they have a panicky ten minutes wondering whether they should go ahead themselves.

An alternative is facial acupuncture, which was used as a beauty tool for hundreds, if not thousands, of years by the empresses of China. Practitioners claim that facial acupuncture stimulates collagen production, helps minimize the appearance of fine lines, reduces the depth of deeper lines and improves skin tone, but whereas Botox freezes muscles this form of treatment can stimulate and revitalize them.

Facial acupuncture also reviews and addresses the internal reasons for poor skin or premature aging by stimulating the function of organs such as the heart and the liver and helping to improve digestion. Patients report additional medical benefits, including a resurgence of energy and improvements in circulation. It's well worth investigating as an alternative to the dreaded cosmetic surgery.

(v: Necessary vanity)

~

BOUNCING BACK

The ability to draw a line underneath an unhappy event and move on is the thing to aim for.

(v: Bereavement, Depression, Despair, Grief, I don't)

~

BOUNDARIES

Boundaries can encompass personal space, emotional vulnerability, legal rights, or simply the right not to let anybody else use your toothpaste. Strong boundary setting is seen as a cornerstone of a healthy relationship. People who are very good at setting boundaries are often confused with people who are just very good at getting their own way by those who are not very good at setting boundaries. But if in doubt make a list of the behaviors of those around you that are repetitive, intrusive and get you down, e.g. interrupting while you are on the phone, leaving dirty clothes on the floor, smoking weed in the living room or not taking their turn to put out the garbage, and decide to do something about it. People don't like changing so be prepared to face criticism, anger and possibly even derision – but don't be derailed. Keeping calm while remaining assertive and polite, but at the same time sticking to your guns, is what boundary setting is all about.

(v: Anger, Codependency, Taboos)

✺

BOYFRIENDS
It's nice having a boyfriend but it's not essential
to your happiness.

✺

BOY TOYS
*'How absurd and delicious it is to be in love with
somebody younger than yourself. Everybody should try it.'*
– BARBARA PYM

Up to a point. You should be aware that there is nothing more grim than a woman of a certain age trotting about with someone who looks like a nephew or a male au pair. Yes, we hear you cry. Men can do it so what the hell? True. But more often than not these guys are trophy buffers or tax-dodging exiles from their country of origin, signing very large checks for pneumatic women who have to fake orgasm. And pity the doll who is caught with the fella who looks like her son's best friend. The likelihood is that in the short term it may put the va back into your va-va-voom. But the upkeep is exhausting and suggests a battleship-load of maintenance just to keep yourself in the frame. In the long run, it's all a bit of regional soap opera as opposed to *Tender Is the Night*.

∾

BOXING

Traditionally associated with the male of the species, after *Million Dollar Baby* came along it became commonplace to see women boxing at the gym. It may not suit all of us, but it turns out that boxing can be fun. It's a focused way of releasing aggression (or, in turn, discovering it) in a safe environment. It is also particularly good for core strength, upper arms, busts and, very importantly – waists. Check out what your local gym has to offer boxing-wise: either one-on-one or a boxing class. If you discover that you enjoy it, invest in a good pair of boxing gloves. You don't have to 'enter the ring' to reap the benefits, but it's pleasing to know that, if necessary, your right hook is up to scratch.

(v: Ballooning weight, Helen Mirren, Waist)

 denote

BRAS

According to the experts, we've nearly all got it wrong in the brassiere department. Apparently 76% of the female population wear ill-fitting bras every day and probably have drawers full of wrong 'uns. The most common mistake is to buy a bra with too big a back and too small cuppage. This can be dire as it pushes the bosom outwards as opposed to inwards.

Sadly, we have also discovered that even weight changes will not help you remold the bosom. So it's simple. Get a fitting! Most good stores offer this service. If you are over 35 invest proper money in two good bras. We promise you won't regret it.

(v: Boobs, Creative corsetry, I can't afford to buy cheap)

denote

BRAZILIAN

'It's the leaf around the flower, the lawn around the house.
You have to love hair in order to love the vagina.'
– *THE VAGINA MONOLOGUES*, EVE ENSLER

(v: Hairiness, Pornification)

denote

BREAST-FEEDING

We are not going to go into the practicalities but it's clearly important and fulfilling to breast-feed if you can – sixteen weeks is a good target. However, if you can't, and there are myriad reasons why it may not be possible, don't beat yourself up about it. What a baby needs most is a calm mother who is getting enough sleep, not an exhausted and strung-out harpy angsting about whether her baby is getting enough milk or when the World Health Organization says it's the right time to start weaning. There are plenty of well-balanced strapping young men (and women) brought up on formula milk and tinned chocolate pudding to prove the point.

(v: Allergies, Babies, Boobs, Implants)

BROTHERS

You can feel incredibly close and familial with your brothers when you see them but at the same time also very far away. They are, after all, blokes and as soon as childhood is left behind their daily concerns and interests may be very different from yours. Once they have steady girlfriends or settle down with a partner or wife you will have to make every effort to include his partner as that may be a vital route through which to remain connected to your brother.

However, although you may not talk to your brothers every day they can play a very important role in your life and you in theirs. They can help you think like a man, particularly in matters of the heart. They can tell it to you straight when others cannot (after all, they know you very well indeed). They can offer measured advice in a way that an overcontrolling overanxious father may not be able to do and they can offer insight and support if you find yourself alone bringing up teenage boys. In

the long term, a good relationship with brothers, indeed with all
your siblings, is vital if you find that you have to make diffcult
decisions about the care of elderly parents. Much depends on
whether you actually like each other beyond loving each other
and to a certain extent that is in the lap of the gods.

(v: Family therapy, Teenagers, Think like a man)

ᜐᜈ

BULLYING

Bullying is generally associated with childhood and adolescence
but adults can bully people too. Bullies are generally people who
at some level feel insecure, overcompetitive, inadequate, intensely
jealous of others and unloved, however successful they may or may
not be. Bullies can just be copying others because they are too
immature or too stupid to take an independent view themselves.
However, if you are a victim of bullying all you can see in your
oppressor is the tyrannical, manipulative, unpleasant aspects of his
or her nature. It's deeply unpleasant and often very frightening.
Sadly, bullying at work and at home is common, and mothers take
note, if you face, and put up with, a barrage of criticism every day
from your children you may well be being bullied. The first step
is to confront the bully and set some boundaries about the future,
but to do this you may need professional support.

(v: Boundaries, Codependency, Domestic violence, Sexual harassment)

BUNDLING

This is a term to describe going to bed with somebody who you probably quite fancy but in the event decide by mutual agreement not to have sex. You may cuddle and kiss and chat for a bit but then you bundle up together and go to sleep. But be warned, you may end up pissed off after all.

(v: Bachelors)

BYE-BYE BABY

Yes. This is tough. Yes it hurts but you have to be brave. When your children leave home, of course, you will feel the loss of the baby you fed on the hour, every hour and loved and hugged so much. You will probably spend several days, if not weeks, wandering round the house feeling like a giant electric socket without a plug and wondering, 'Where did the time go and what is left to me?'. You never stop being a parent. At the same time, mists clear, horizons beckon and you will discover a new independence.

(v: Adventure, Babies, Infinite vistas)

CAMIKNICKERS

Our grandmothers knew what they were up to. Classic but sexy, comfortable, practical and flattering, camiknickers are a wardrobe essential. Buy them in light colors: cream, pale pink, violet blue and silver-grey . . . darker colors can be ageing, with the exception of red. Red camiknickers are particularly cheering in winter. If this sounds extravagant, see the glossary for e-shops that do an excellent and reasonably priced range. Camiknickers will cover lumpy bottoms, make thighs look trim and, most importantly, wearing them will give you secret confidence.

(v: Affairs, Cinq à sept, Creative corsetry, Secret confidence)

CANCELING CHRISTMAS
'Have a great Christmas, but only if you want to.'
– ROB RAYNER

It is okay to do this unless you have very young children. This time of year can be a very difficult and stressful and lonely time for many people. One way of getting around it is to volunteer to do charitable work and encourage your lazy parents to join in, i.e. helping the homeless, or deprived or traumatized children, or housebound old folk have some kind of Christmas. This means that you are doing something worthwhile, you will actually enjoy yourself and you are avoiding the hideous materialism that epitomizes the Christmas season. However, it has become increasingly fashionable to volunteer and so you may find your offer of help is turned down. Don't be downhearted as you are now entirely within your rights to fly to the nearest non-Christian country and stay there for some time, but do think about offering your services to a local charity in a more sustainable way in the New Year.

(v: Going to prison, Hell, Volunteering)

∽∾

CANCER BUDDY

Cancer is virtually a pandemic in the Western world. The likelihood is that one in three of us will get some form of cancer during our lifetime and may even die of it. Breast cancer is the commonest form of cancer in women so you will probably know somebody who has it, has had it, or you may even be a sufferer yourself. The good news is that the treatment of breast cancer has been so broadly successful that the disease has been reclassified as a chronic illness rather than a life-threatening disease, but whichever way you look at it cancer is not fun and chemotherapy and radiotherapy can leave patients feeling more ill, more exhausted and more demoralized than when they were first given their diagnosis. Whether you are becoming a cancer buddy, or are looking for one, the job description is as follows:

1. This is not about you. However upset you are that your friend is ill you must put those feelings to one side and concentrate on your friend and her family.

2. A regular commitment to spending time looking after your friend is a nice offer. Don't just say I'll do anything to help, plan ahead and come up with a variety of suggestions – whether it's accompanying her to hospital while she undergoes chemotherapy, taking her to see a movie or simply suggesting a walk in the park on a sunny day. Let your friend choose.

3. Lovely surprise gifts such as flowers, scented candles or cozy bed socks will be greatly appreciated but don't forget practical tasks too. Offering to make a meal, clean the house (chemotherapy patients are very susceptible to infections), walk the dog, drive the car, or pick up the kids can be as blessed as a bottle of delicious scent.

4. Having cancer is boring. If your friend wants to talk about it ad infinitum it's fine but your job is to be cheerful, life-enhancing and try to normalize what can be a grave situation. It's important to inject some fun into the proceedings and if your friend is bedridden some good gossip can be very diverting indeed.

5. Be sensitive to the needs of her family and other friends. Don't monopolize your friend or take control of her life, requests or requirements, or, worst of all, become competitive with your friend's other cancer buddies. Sometimes the best thing you can do is just to leave a flask of soup by the door.

6. Remember to celebrate any good news your friend may receive, and there will be some in the course of treatment, even if the long-term prognosis isn't great.

7. You are allowed to feel sadness too but you need to take responsibility for this and process it at home.

(v: Hair loss, Hospital etiquette, Leaving the party,
Making a will, Memory boxes, Ward wear)

❧

CANDLES

In almost all faiths, votive candles are part of ritual observances. In modern times there is something incredibly cheering and festive, particularly in the depths of winter, about taking the time to light strategically placed candles around the house. The clutter disappears, ditto the cat hair, the peeling paintwork. You don't even have to wait until twilight falls, in Scandinavia candles are lit at any time of the day or night.

However, a word of warning. Candles – like cushions – are a girl thing. Men are baffled by them. And yes, you can have too many in a household. As columnist Julie Burchill hilariously observed, 'I bet you could prove with pie charts that the more scented candles a woman buys, the less orgasms/job security she has.' Ouch.

(v: Magic spells)

ത

CAN'T

Or won't? 'There is no such word as can't.' If you ever find yourself saying, 'but I can't . . .', simply replace the phrase with 'I'll try', unless your personal safety is at risk or your actions will deeply hurt somebody you love. The results can be extraordinary.

(v: I don't)

ത

CARBOHYDRATES

Nowadays it's socially acceptable to have a glass of wine or dabble in illicit substances but should one piece of bread pass your lips you know that you will be damned for all eternity.

Boring though it is to have to admit it, and although in theory we don't believe in dieting, ditching the carbs does help knock off the pounds. This basically means doing the Atkins, without doing the Atkins. Or doing a sort of Atkins, but with a tiny bit of carbs on the side. It still works.

Carbs are also addictive, so the less you eat them, the less you want them. This will help you keep the weight off once you have lost it. So let's reframe the idea of 'dieting' as 'slightly changing the way you eat' and we'll throw in some super-foods too for good measure. Why the hell not?

(v: Ballooning weight, Blueberries, Diets, Eat your greens,
Going to prison, Waist)

༒

CARS

It's less important if you live in a city but if you are single and want a car, you need to have a man who knows his carburetor who you can go to and wring your hands and say, 'Can you sort this out please, as I have to go away, ooh, and by the way I don't have much money'. It's counterintuitive feminism. The 'damsel in distress' is usually a very good turn where a jalopy is concerned, simply because men love to be macho and practical, and they also love to help out. This is the perfect conduit for their frustrations. Having said that, please don't forget to sign up with the Automobile Association or equivalent. If you discover that the aforementioned male doesn't know his carburetor from. his callipers then the AAA will prove invaluable.

Many women bang on about cars being unnecessary, but they are vital if you want to visit friends in the country and/or have kids and generally buzz about the city not carrying a coat.

(v: Counterintuitive feminism, Taxis)

༒

CASUAL SEX

An awful lot of moralistic drivel is written about casual sex. Ultimately it's your choice.

(v: Bachelors, Booty calls, Contraception,
It's a gift, No sex before marriage, Twice is polite)

CATCHING THE BOUQUET

If 27 is the new 18 then the age limit for bridesmaids has risen exponentially. What was the preserve of tiny tots, your best friend from school, your sisters and virgins or at least the unmarried is now open to pretty much anyone of any age – not least your newly divorced godmother. So let's not be ageist about bridesmaiding. Choose the women, whatever their age, you love best to accompany you through the preparation for the profound ceremony of marriage and don't forget that nowadays no single woman is too old to catch the bouquet. However, if you feel you are really too elderly to totter down the aisle in peach chiffon behind your three-times-already married best friend you are allowed to say so.

(v: BFF, Wearing white dresses, Wedding cake)

CATNAPPING

Whether you are a cat, a master of the universe, a cockney sparrow or Spanish having a siesta, having a power snooze, having a little lie-down, taking a nap, taking forty winks, sleeping in the afternoon is one of the joys of life. It is restorative in every sense. An hour in the afternoon is worth about three hours sleep at night, and can take the edge off exhaustion, lift your spirits and prepare you for a long night out.

(v: Bolt-hole)

CATS

Forget clichés about elderly spinsters in shapeless housecoats with cat hair in the butter, cat owners are true sensualists. You get a graceful, tactile, independent admirer in four-legged form. Cats are pretty low maintenance: they don't mind you going out to work – and they do wonders for your physical and mental well-being. Relationships with cats are (largely) free of the psychological games inherent in human relationships. Pets don't have mood swings or meltdowns and they never talk back. They are great levelers. Plus, they're elegant. Cats are supergroomers – and never have a bad-hair day.

It's often better to get two kittens. They are company for each other and not much more expensive. Or, if you don't have time for rearing young cats, choosing an older, house-trained moggie from a pet rescue center is a great solution. Never give them embarrassing names (cats have their pride). And do invest in pet insurance from day one. Just make sure their dental bills aren't higher than yours!

(v: Blow-dries, Hope)

CAVEMAN MOMENT

We all have to admit to having a caveman moment from time to time. That swoony guy who could surely sling you over his shoulder, gather wood, make a fire and then go and kill something for dinner with no mucking about reading poetry to you either. *Grr.* The thing is, he is often quite cavemanish in other respects too. So after the initial swooning and OMG moments, you are left with, er, a caveman. We all love a hunk who can chop down a trunk but in the cold light of a twenty-first-century dawn we may decide we need other qualities in a man for a longer-lasting relationship.

(v: Bitches and hos, Fur,)

CHAMPAGNE

'I drink it when I'm happy
And when I'm sad.
Sometimes I drink it when I'm alone.
When I have company I consider it obligatory.
I trifle with it if I'm not hungry
And I drink it when I am.
Otherwise I never touch it, unless I'm thirsty.'
– MADAME LILY BOLLINGER

Let's also raise a glass to the heroic Madame Clicquot Ponsardin who in 1805, aged 27, took over the company on her husband's death and developed the now ubiquitous Veuve Clicquot. How extremely clever and very progressive of her to use her widowhood to name and brand her champagne, restore her family fortunes and give so many people so much pleasure down the ages.

(v: Booze, Cocktails, Dipsomania, Drunk-dialing)

CHARM

Is a double-edged sword.

(v: Bachelors)

CHASTITY

It has become fashionable to opt for chastity as a way of protecting oneself from potential abuse and subsequent heartbreak at the hands of the hordes of emotionally inadequate men who roam our streets and frequent our parties. But you do have a choice, so exercise it.

Don't go to bed with a man who you know isn't going to be nice to you in the morning.

(v: Entering a convent, No sex before marriage)

CHEATING

In card games or life cheating has an underhanded quality that is deeply unattractive. It suggests a desire to win whatever the cost and an inability to respect fine qualities and genuine abilities in others. Cheats tend to be found out, cf. Lord Jeffrey Archer, Lord Conrad Black, Bernie Madoff, and are universally despised except by other cheats. Women tend to cheat with a little more style and a great deal more sex appeal, cf. M'Lady in *The Three Musketeers* and Mata Hari, and so we can forgive them almost anything.

(v: Poker)

〜

CHESS

Alongside crossword puzzles and sudoku, chess exercises the functions of the junctions and stimulates the neural paths in one's brain. Allegedly this prevents Alzheimer's. It's probably worth a try.

〜

CHILDBIRTH

Quite a lot of fuss is made about childbirth.

(v: Fertility, Five Element acupuncture, Pregnancy, Ward wear)

〜

CHILDFREE

One in five women aged 45 is now childfree. Analysts suggest both men and women want to work and play harder for longer before settling down. For some, it's enough of a challenge to meet a significant other for cocktails and minibreaks, let alone think about rearing a child together, but the good news is that being childfree – a far more positive phrase than childless – is now quite socially acceptable.

There are a number of women who actively choose not to have children. They prefer to put their lover, their job and their freedom first and not everyone craves the traditional nuclear family or is automatically maternal.

If you don't have children, there is more time for holidays, parties, time-consuming hobbies and enduring friendships and the right to have fun – and yes, to be selfish – without apology. It's also increasingly seen as a green choice.

But it is still an issue of pain for many. Fertility is never a given, so smug parents please go gently, plus becoming childfree can creep up on you while you are busy doing other things. It isn't necessarily a conscious decision. It's hard to know exactly when you're grown-up enough to be a parent – or even to be in a committed relationship. Men, bless them, will always have a get-out clause but the risk for women of starting (or ending) relationships later in life is that you may find it's too late to sprog.

(v: Aunts, Babies, Quests, Termination)

✺

CHOCOLATE

Handmade artisan chocolate is the new Châteauneuf-du-Pape. New waves of chocolatiers are cooking up extraordinary flavors – everything from chocolate with chili to pineapple confit with ylang-ylang – in their laboratories. It has become the grown-up dinner party gift of choice.

All of us deserve decent chocolate, but for those of you worrying about ballooning weight the mantra is eat less but eat better. A single, exquisite, jasmine-tea truffle is better value than a box of brand-name chocolates. The higher the cocoa content (70% plus is good), the less sugar and saturated fat it contains.

Chocolate gets bad press (mostly from men), but chocolate is also the reward you give yourself when life is going badly. It's the perfect way to cancel out a bad date, to calm a hangover or simply to grab supper on the run. Chocolate has amazing flavor and complexity, and it's the only form of nourishment that melts at body temperature. More emotion is invested in chocolate than any other foodstuff: it has a Proustian interplay with memory, perception and fantasy. It makes you friends and takes you out of yourself.

Chocolate can be deeply sexy too.

(v: Ballooning weight, Diet)

cr

CHOIRS

Forget cabaret or stand-up, choirs are one of the best ways to meet new people. At the end of the evening you can all pile into the café or pub, you get to travel to performances and competitions, and you will learn to love being part of an ensemble, something bigger than yourself. And there is the sheer physical joy of singing.

Choirs are democratic. Every person brings a different dynamic to the group and the interaction between you – on a personal and social level – sets you apart from any other kind of band. It's the exact opposite of an *X Factor* audition. Memories of school choir practice might put you off, especially if you couldn't read sheet music and were asked to mime, but with the new 'indie' or 'scratch' choirs, it doesn't matter if you're not formally trained.

Communal singing is a powerful way to bond. With indie choirs, you don't have to turn up to millions of rehearsals. Often the call goes out via Facebook and what could be more human and more fun than a bunch of people shedding their ordinary lives to meet once a week to make music?

(v: Churches, Flow, Get out of a rut and get involved)

CHURCHES

Don't walk on by. Glorious stained glass windows. Total sanctuaries with spellbinding architecture. Curiously soothing haven to just drop by and take in. Pray to your God, whoever they may be. The welcome mat is always out.

(v: Choirs, Flow, Get out of a rut and get involved)

CIDER VINEGAR

A teaspoon in a cup of hot water is regarded by many as the absolute dream ticket to reboot and make you bright eyed and perky. Quaff on a twice-daily basis and true believers swear you will shrink and glow with good health.

(v: Climacteric, Diets, Skin)

CINQ À SEPT

The magic time between five and seven p.m. (as the phrase denotes) when lovers meet. The phrase was invented by Parisians. Moral concerns aside, by leaving work a little early you will still have enough time to make your assignation and then get home in order to shower, change and sit down to supper with your respective partners. You will discover too that afternoon sex has its own particular pleasures and rewards.

(v: Affairs, Arrangement, Creative corsetry, Twice is polite)

ॐ

CLEANING
'Behind every immaculate house is a very dull person.'
– ANONYMOUS

Cleaning is both overrated and underrated. A little mess here and there, plus a couple of cobwebs, never did anybody any harm. However, if you want to create a bit of mental space there is nothing quite like a calm, well-ordered home.

(v: Allergies, Flow, Housework, Infinite vistas)

ॐ

(TO) CLEANSE OR NOT TO CLEANSE
Choose a product gentle enough for your skin. You are trying to remove oil and retain water (moisture) – something too strong will dry your skin out and stimulate oil glands to produce more. The trick is to apply heat (a warm cloth) to your pores so oil can be melted otherwise it will stay under the first layer of skin – and you'll get spots.

Morning or night, a good dollop of cleanser massaged into your skin, in upward and outward circular movements, and removed with a warm muslin cloth leaves it clean and revived. The cloth helps gently exfoliate your skin's surface.

(v: Beauty industry)

ᘉ

(The) Climacteric (menopause)

Oceans has been written about this period of transformation in a woman's life and we provide some reading suggestions in the bibliography. Some people hardly notice 'the Change', for others it's a grueling and miserable experience that can come with huge physical discomfort and emotional upset. However, the key thing is to understand that it is not an illness and that an awful lot can be done to help if symptoms are acute. Diet and exercise can play their part and if you are contemplating hormone replacement therapy, we urge you to research bio-identical hormone replacement therapy instead.

(v: Contraception, Eat your greens, Fertility)

ᘉ

Cocktails

'One is perfect. Two is too many. Three is not enough.'
– James Thurber

Cocktails are girl heaven, an escape from what Kingsley Amis once described as the three most depressing words in the English language, 'red or white'. Cocktails give confidence and class – and take the edge off a dull day or a difficult everything. There's always an excuse to sink a strawberry daiquiri with a girlfriend. It can be like starring in your own private film and there's a whiff of danger too. Cocktails were invented during Prohibition in the United States in the 1920s and drunk secretly in speakeasys.

Even today, the best bars remain discreet and the American TV series *Mad Men* has made cocktail drinking cool again. Back in fashion are strong-tasting spirits – bourbon, rye whiskey and gin – made using classic recipes with a modern twist. But don't be apologetic if you yearn for creamy concoctions with paper umbrellas and Carmen Miranda–style fruit garnishes. Long drinks can be better for the wallet – and the head.

Decor is crucial. Old-school sophistication is what you are looking for. Champagne bars at railway stations inspire childlike enthusiasm: but don't meet up on the day you're supposed to actually catch a train.

There are a few ground rules for the great last-minute cocktail fling. Dress up. Remember to eat or the waiters will regret letting you through the velvet rope. And do watch those rounds. Beauty comes at a price. You may be sitting in art deco heaven, but then most cocktails will start at a minimum of $15 each. And however much you are tempted, we really don't recommend drinking more than two or, at a stretch three, in one sitting – unless of course you are on a bender.

(v: Alcohol, Bad habits, Benders, Bombshells, Booze, Champagne, Dipsomania, Drunk-dialing)

◠

CODEPENDENCY

A term that is bandied about a great deal, sometimes jokingly. However, it is worth understanding what it means and how it might be affecting you. Addiction is a family disease and codependents are people who find themselves in relationships with people who are alcoholic or drug dependent. There are over fifty varieties of addiction and while codependents may not be addicts themselves, there may be a family history of addiction. Codependents sometimes, though not always, have also suffered from some form of abuse or grievous loss at an early age that enables them to develop highly sophisticated coping mechanisms to face the world, but which overlay great suffering and vulnerability. To the outside world, codependents may appear to be highly functioning, successful and extremely charming, but secretly they can suffer from a crippling lack of self-worth and be super critical of themselves and others. In their efforts to keep control of the deteriorating family situation they find themselves in they may actually enable the addict in his or her addiction.

(v: Dipsomania)

ოღა

Cognitive behavioral therapy (CBT)

Is very à la mode in therapeutic circles and is a useful tool if you want to change repetitive and depressive thinking and destructive patterns of behavior. It's essentially about pressing the reset button.

(v: Depression, Visualization)

~

COLD SHOWERS

The infamous Scandinavian secret is the power shower, which jump-starts the system and makes you run like a Duracell bunny. Can and should become a serious habit.

(v: Skin)

~

COLOR

We rather took the mickey out of Color Me Beautiful image consultants at the time when it was launched but in retrospect it's an extremely useful tool. The sight of armies of students, office workers and shoppers clad in unrelenting funereal black is drab. So bring back the sixties and rock on flower power.

Popping colors can give you zing and totally alter your mood, as well other people's. Prints and tangerines are prettier to look at, full stop. Everybody has certain colors that really work with their shade of hair and skin tone, so it is worth finding out if it is turquoise, scarlet, violet, canary yellow or lime green that works for you. Color is a tonic all round. Not for nothing is shocking pink called the navy blue of India. If you can't say goodbye to darker tones, lighten up a charcoal grey cardigan with a dazzling scarf or a pair of red tights. We dare you.

(v: Bombshell)

ᘓᖇᑎ

COMFORT ZONE
'Life begins at the end of your comfort zone.'
– NEALE DONALD WALSCH [AUTHOR]

We all need to get out of our comfort zone. Getting damp and chilly is one of the best ways of making you feel alive. We spend far too much time grumbling about the weather while lurking in our cozy, heated office or home 'pods', where the worst thing that can happen is that a heel snaps. Getting on a horse, jumping in a river, rowing a boat, sleeping outdoors in a tent, these are all ways of getting back to basics and out of your comfort zone. Reaching a destination, cold and wet, after a hard and taxing journey, is lovely and will make you feel both challenged and proud. Even walking up the stairs to the office is, for many, a goal achieved. If you live in the country there is no excuse. If you are a city dweller, you still have access to parks, where all sorts of organized activities can be found, whether hiking, riding, rowing or bicycling. But whatever your plan, ensure there is a hot shower and a decent supper at the end of it.

(v: Adventure, Flow)

ᘓᖇᑎ

COMPANIONSHIP
'It is the friends you can call up at 4 a.m. that matter.'
– MARLENE DIETRICH

Companions are part of the joyous sense of our lives. They know what makes us tick and what makes us laugh and they travel alongside us. Romantic love can be selfish – 'I want you alone' – while companionship means making the most of the time two people have, not just for being together, but togetherness.

The truth is companionship is just as important as sex. Ask most couples why they chose their life partner, and they'll most likely answer, 'We enjoy each other's company'. It is impossible to foresee what our interests and likes and dislikes will be twenty years down the road – people mature differently – but the true measure of companionship is one's ability to accept development and change in a friend or partner without feeling it threatens us in any way.

There is nothing worse than feeling 'uncompanionable'. It is arguably more upsetting than a lover's tiff. We take pride in our friends, pleased that they have chosen us and that we have chosen them. They 'get' us and reinforce our sense of self.

(v: BFF, Good husband material)

๛

COMPLAIN

The service is bad. The food is revolting. The shop assistant is rude. Your face is puce, your heart is pounding, you feel resentful and you want to throw something through the window. Don't! Transfer the guilt back to the shop/service/annoying thing in hand, and merely ask, 'How can they make this up to me?'. Embellish naturally (a woman's prerogative), 'I bought this for my mother/It's my birthday/I'm going away tomorrow' . . . that sort of thing. One of the few upsides of the Big Brother age is that all companies are now hidebound by recorded conversations and fear bad press from even the most lowly of customers. So stay calm. Take control. Insist on speaking to a manager! Don't take it out on the ill-paid, powerless employee who has the awful task of trying to please you over the phone. Remember courtesy and good behavior at all times, but you do deserve that upgrade. Ask!

(v: Counterintuitive feminism, Good behavior)

COMPLETE WANKERS

Quite a rare beast but if you come across one of these men you will know instantly that you have. Their defining characteristic is that they have no redeeming qualities whatsoever. Don't bother to argue with them, it's a waste of your extremely valuable time. Make your excuses and leave at the earliest available opportunity.

(v: Committed bachelors, Emergency exit, Narcissus)

CONDOMS

You know your options. In these days of snazzy new contraceptive devices (implants under the skin of your arm, indeed!), it's easy to overlook the simple, practical chic of the condom. Safe to use, they are cheap and easy to obtain.

Being prepared doesn't make you a slut. Carrying condoms shows a willingness to practice safe sex and shows respect for a partner's and your own sexual health. Stash a pack in your handbag and simply forget about them until needed. Do occasionally check that they are not expired.

Barrier contraception is key at any age because it not only protects you from unwanted pregnancies, but also from a number of very much unwanted STDs. It's important that you protect and survive especially if you are dating casually. Be assertive: you know what's best for your body so say exactly how you feel.

Don't let anyone sweet-talk you into having sex without a condom because 'it feels better'. Put bluntly: if it's not on – it's not in, and wave goodbye to that man if he tries to make life difficult.

(v: Contraception, It's a gift, STDs)

෨

Confidence

'There's no mystery to confidence, it's just about self knowledge. It's savvy to know which of our flaws can be changed, and which ones to accept and let go. Then, making the best of the good points.'
– IMMODESTY BLAIZE [ICON]

It is the heart of the matter. If you are genuinely confident you remain unflustered about what other people think of you, are interested in the outside world, can be open about your feelings, but are not seeking approval from others.

(v: Bien dans ta peau, Necessary vanity, Secret confidence)

~

CONTAINER GARDENS

All you need is outside space – anything from a window box to a balcony or a yard, where you can have planters and troughs. The more low maintenance the better.

There's no point in having anything that you will under- or overwater or will be kicked up by boys, dogs or footballs. No fragile blooms. No succulents. Stick to drought-resistant plants.

The joy of a container garden is that if there's room it's like having an extra room in the house, which you can decorate with chairs, a table or chaise longue. Plants can be grown in virtually anything, provided you add some drainage holes. We've seen herbs growing in shoes and rows of beans sprouting from upturned hats. Recycle old suitcases, sinks and trunks too.

Plus there is the sheer joy of walking around a garden center. Forget the plants, it's the people. There's something rather wonderful about watching folk from opposite sides of the class divide bonding over cottage garden flowers.

But just don't expect all your green-fingered friends to approve of your new container 'scheme'. They'll remark that the *Fatsia* is unhappy or insist that New Zealand grasses might have been a better choice. Don't forget that gardening can be the sport of the *Borgias*.

❧

CONTRACEPTION

(v: Condoms, It's a gift, STDs)

❧

CONTROL FREAKS

They love to impose their beliefs and foibles onto others and therefore are often draining company. The 'live and let live' ethos passes them by as they go about their business, bossily policing people's lives, going through their bins, metaphorical or otherwise, and giving a great deal of unsought advice. But beware. There's a little bit of a control freak waiting to ignite in all of us and once it takes hold it's a very hard habit to break. Step back while you can and begin to listen more instead.

(v: Advice, Bullying, Codependency, Dangers of overplanning,
Exquisite listening)

❧

CONVERSATION (ART OF)

Agh. The art of small talk. The *je ne sais quoi*. Sadly, unlike politicians and state leaders, we don't all get furtively briefed with a finely honed precis, such as, 'This is Matthew. He's a spy and likes jumping on and off trains and making quick exits from hotels', which is, of course, potentially riveting. No. Mere mortals such as ourselves have to take our courage in both hands and pretend that we are wholly comfortable with the social scenario we find ourselves inhabiting, however unconfident we may feel. If one is feeling very shy, a good way of protecting one's inner core is to be extremely charming and ask questions of and be totally interested in other people. It turns out that everybody secretly loves talking about themselves and they will be very flattered by your interest in them. Let them. Inquire, make jokes, be self-deprecating. You will seem gracious and relaxed and if there is a dread pause in the conversation, 'Can I get you another drink?' always works very well too.

(v: Be well informed, Bores, Self-confidence, Small talk)

COOKING
Ready, steady, yes. This is what women the
world over do several times a day.

(v: Anna Del Conte)

COSMETIC SURGERY
(v: Climacteric, Diets, Facial acupuncture, Tummy tuck)

COUNTERINTUITIVE FEMINISM
Essentially female behavior that may look atavistic but which masks an iron will to ensure that you get your own way in the end.

(v: Cars, Mrs. Thatcher)

⋐⋒⋑

COUNTRY WEEKENDS (WEEKEND RETREATS)

Even if you weren't born with a title and a trust fund, you can always jump the class barrier and stage your very own *Great Gatsby* house party – as long as your chosen destination has a long drawing room for pre-dinner drinks, four-poster beds and a croquet lawn. City dwellers often underestimate the rejuvenating power of a weekend away. The minute you hit the motorway, your spirits will lift at the prospect of rolling countryside, long walks and roaring fires. A word of warning about the country, however, it's very green. There are no shops and to get mobile phone reception you probably have to climb on top of a barn. Plus, if you're staying in someone else's country house, there's a bewildering etiquette to learn. Should you help yourself to breakfast in the morning? How do you light a fire? How do you address the housekeeper? The key to getting it right with your hosts is to bring at least a couple of bottles of decent wine, an additional present such as some lovely soap or a slim volume of verse and always, always, always write a proper thank-you letter. Arguably the more 'natural' and at ease with yourself you are, the more rewarding the country experience will be. Even uptight townies unwind in the end. Climb a hill, get muddy, swim in a river: you'll come back glowing with health, having spent a weekend in an elegant bubble, only smelling slightly of wet dog.

(v: Bolt-hole, Comfort zone, Courtesy, Guests, Seaside)

COURTESY

A little of this can go a very long way; and there are certain key attitudes that even a postfeminist man should adhere to. If common courtesy could be rolled out around the world, what a sweeter place it would be.

To have the door opened with the words 'No, after you', is a delight. An instant 'Let me take that for you', at the sight of a woman struggling with bags of shopping and staggering to the bus or car is music to our ears. Asking 'How are you getting home?', 'Shall I call you a cab?' and then walking you to the aforementioned cab (and opening the door) earns a man five gold stars.

This may sound like charm-school stuff, but it used to be a blueprint for male behavior across society. In particular, we despair that men no longer get up for pregnant women on busy subways and trains. So how do we bring common courtesy back? Answers on a postcard please.

(v: Manners, Twice is polite)

CRASH PADS

You're on to date number five. After a movie, supper and flirting, you suggest going back to his place.

The date looks into your eyes and says coolly, 'Damn it, let's get a hotel!'

Crash-pad hotels are the latest trend. Instead of trekking

home on public transport, you can check into a chic boutique hotel without breaking the bank. If all is going well you won't have had a decent night's sleep and you'll arrive unfashionably late at the office, but if the reverse you can at least console yourself that you've gone to work early looking revived and refreshed and will impress your boss.

The crash-pad model is based on no-frills time-share-style hotels – the sort you get at airports or train stations. But it has none of the seedy associations of the 1970's shag pad. You'll get a state-of-the-art entertainment system, mini bar and even a New York–style wet room.

Instead of worrying about how tidy your bedroom is, or whether you've got anything to drink at home, you can focus on pure pleasure. Frazzled couples who have managed to get a babysitter for the night might even want to book in for the whole evening.

The unspoken message of the crash pad is clear: you are here, only briefly, to rest and recharge. Everyone deserves to feel like a rock star for a night.

(v: Creative corsetry)

~

CREATIVE CORSETRY

Every over-40-something Oscar-winning actress and mother of three is bending over backwards (literally) to be on the cover of *Vanity Fair* wearing a corset and garters and not much else, claiming that she's beginning to explore the dark side of her sexuality. We blame Madonna. So to remind you of the rules, this kind of kit is only to be worn onstage at the Folies Bergère in Paris or Caesar's Palace in Las Vegas or in the privacy of your own bedroom or hotel room.

(v: Affairs, Crash pads, Have you got the kit?, Pornography)

CREDIT CARDS

We all have a love-hate relationship with credit cards. On the one hand they enable us to buy beautiful and expensive shoes, on the other they highlight the poisonous relationship between 'consumers' (by the way, when did we stop being people?) and banks. If you find yourself in trouble with a credit card, and many of us do, there isn't an excuse. You need to face the problem, respond quickly, work out a payment plan, set up a standing order and stick to your budget. And don't forget to cut the card up.

(v: Grasping the nettle, Money matters, Opening brown envelopes)

CRISIS

When you are having a meltdown it's annoying to be told by the office know-it-all that in Chinese the word crisis also means opportunity. However, there is a grain of truth in this old adage so instead of kicking the door in or sitting down to write a suicide note, think about the dramatic and sometimes positive alternatives that a crisis might be offering you. Whether it's the abrupt end of an increasingly unsatisfactory relationship, losing a job that ultimately you don't like very much or facing bankruptcy, you are finally being forced to confront problems that have probably been simmering away for quite some time. This could be liberation.

(v: Opportunity, Suicide)

ᘒ

CROSS-GENERATIONAL FRIENDSHIP

These days it's not unusual to see a 38-year-old and a 70-year-old having dinner together. We are all beginning to understand it is unhealthy to hang out exclusively with your own age group. A true friend is someone who makes you think differently, who is willing to share the risks that any increase in complexity brings – that's why cross-generational friendships are so rewarding. It's important to look beyond your obvious social group.

Older friends bring wisdom and perspective and teach you not to waste time on regrets. They tend to be less judgemental and less competitive. There's very little they haven't lived through, and they enjoy your strengths. Plus, they can be a humbling reminder to us that we ain't seen nothing yet when it comes to hedonistic rule breaking.

Younger friends keep us on our toes – whether it's recommending new shops and bars, tweaking our wardrobe, ('yes' to the leather jacket, 'no' to the kitten heels) or teaching us to download the latest apps. As a more assertive generation with liberal parents, they have a refreshing – and surprisingly good – take on sex and love. They are less likely to obsess about work and they understand pleasure. And they take us out of our comfort zone. They do need a bit of guidance and support too, but it's rewarding for us to feel we can reciprocate.

It's a huge compliment to be adopted as a friend by somebody who is twenty years younger or older than you. But no one is asking you to be a neoparent or an old-age pensioner's carer. True cross-generational friendships are fun, not worthy.

(v: BFFs)

CROSSWORDS
(v: Chess, Mental exercise)

CRUSHES

Crushes make the world go round. Anything that puts a sparkle in your eye, makes you brush your hair in the morning and get to work on time, has to be a good thing. Having a crush is like having a pulse – it makes you feel alive.

However, you can't always choose your crushes. Sometimes they just sneak up on you and before you know it – ooh, heavens – who was that?

Adolescent crushes are a trial run for real emotion and a real relationship. They help us understand which qualities we notice and like in another person, and maybe a few that we don't like. If we're older, particularly if we are rendered shy or giddy or tongue-tied by the experience, it can be a nostalgic reminder of teenage rites of passage.

Our crush may never guess the extent of our feelings. Or it might be a mutual crush, where there's a shared but silent acknowledgement that in another life you could have been far more to each other than you are in this one, and there is a pleasurable sadness in acknowledging that. Crushes should be, by definition, a fun flirty pleasure, an escape from real life, or even a tricky patch in a long-term relationship.

But be wary if you find a crush tipping into a full-blown adult obsession. We've probably all been tempted to do a little bit of phone and cyber stalking, cf. Princess Diana, but it rarely ends well. Remember the rules of good behavior still apply.

Likewise, if you're on the receiving end of unrequited attention try to be kind: it's a compliment, but never let anyone behave in a way that makes you feel funny or uncomfortable. That's not a good crush. That's harassment.

Let's not be hypocritical either. Part of the test of crushes for people in long-term relationships is accepting your partner will have them too.

Often we're mortified if the other person realizes we're smitten. But the greater truth is that after the age of 35 everyone loves having admirers. You can never have too much positive attention.

(v: Quests)

ᴖ
CUNT

According to Wikipedia, etymologists cannot completely agree about the origins of the word cunt though it is thought that it is of Norse/German origin and must also bear some relation to the Latin word *cunnus*. It was in common usage during the twelfth century but by the sixteenth century had become a term of abuse. The reasons for this remain unclear but are (presumably) misogynistic in origin. The word appears several times in *The Canterbury Tales*, in a bawdy context, but at this point in its etymological career the word is not considered to be obscene. The main character of *The Wife of Bath's Tale*, who in her own way epitomizes the idea of a Dangerous Woman in the Middle Ages, has this to say on the subject:

'You would have my quente alone?/Wy, taak it al! Lo, have it every deel!/ Peter! I shrewe yow, but you love it weel;/For I wold sell my bele chose, /I kould walke as fresshe as is a rose;/ But I wool kepe it for yor owene tooth.' which translates as:

'Is it because you'd have my cunt alone?/Why take it all, have every bit of it;/Peter! Beshrew you but you're fond of it!/ For if I would go sell my belle chose,/ I could walk out as fresh as is a rose;/But I will keep it for your own sweet tooth.'

Interestingly, after close textual analysis, what looks like a slightly risqué chat reveals a much subtler exploration of the loaded relationship between sex and love, money and power.

Three hundred years later John Donne's sly but loving tribute to the cunt – 'sucked on country pleasures, childishly'–

in the sexy and magnificent sonnet 'The Good Morrow' marks the time when a shadow was beginning to fall on the open use of this word, but whatever it's genus, as Germaine Greer remarks, 'it is one of the few remaining words in the English language that has a genuine power to shock'.

❧

(The) Curse

Old-fashioned slang for menstruation reflects the loaded associations that come with being a daughter of Eve. Luckily advances in science, combined with good vitamin advice and specialist medication combined to make having your period a less onerous task and something that can be talked about in public, though not necessarily at supper.

(v: Menstruation)

❧

Curves

(v: Ballooning weight, Bombshell, Boobs, Creative corsetry, Petticoats)

❧

Cutting ties

'The truth will set you free. But first, it will piss you off.'
– Gloria Steinem

Your time is too precious to spend on people who let you down, jobs that crush your potential or hobbies that you have outgrown.

By all means research the situation carefully first. It would be awful not to give a friend or lover the chance to change. Maybe you can meet halfway so whatever happens you don't burn your bridges. But if when you've thought it through properly and you want to cut ties do it quickly and cleanly. The more quickly you begin the process, the faster it's over. There's no need for bitchiness. You can thank the person for their friendship and say goodbye. But don't look back. It's kinder for everyone – especially you.

(v: Emergency exit)

⟳

CYCLING

Is a fab and practical thing to do, though a challenge if you are whizzing around in a major city surrounded by mad men in garbage trucks. Have clip-on lights and, even though it's not terribly fetching, wear a high-visibility jacket, and a helmet. It's vital you practice your hand signals.

In contrast, cycling in the countryside is a truly blissful way of traveling about, especially in the summertime.

(v: Adventure, Ballooning weight, Flow)

DADDY DAMAGE
'When one has not had a good father, one must create one.'
– FRIEDRICH NIETZSCHE

If only we had world enough and time to do due justice to the
complex relationship between fathers and daughters. At best it
can be an incredibly important paradigm for your future healthy
relationships with men. At worst, and it can get very bad indeed
as the mountains of misery memoirs testify, it can almost
destroy your life. If you feel your present is overshadowed by an
unhappy past, or you find yourself in repetitive patterns when
it comes to relationships with men, it may be that revisiting
past events, in the context of your relationship with your father,
within a therapeutic setting – understanding what happened,
reliving the pain and then moving on – is what will set you free.

(v: Daughters, Family therapy)

 びん

DANCING

'I did everything he did but backwards and in high heels.'

– GINGER ROGERS ON FRED ASTAIRE

(v: Ballroom dancing, Dancing with the devil,
Flow, Tango, Tap dancing)

びん

DANCING WITH THE DEVIL

Go on, take to the floor! You'll need something to talk about in
the old people's home.

(v: Codependency, Control freaks)

びん

DANGERS OF OVERPLANNING

'We must be willing to get rid of the life we've planned,
so as to have the life that is waiting for us.'

– JOSPEH CAMPBELL

Very few people say they enjoy that runaway feeling when
there's so little time and so much to organize, e.g. Christmas,
but are we, in the Western world, in danger of overplanning
our lives away? Is that dreaded but meaningless contemporary
word, 'stress', a modern-day response to atavistic fears that
the world is a frightening and dangerous place, i.e. if you are
worrying in the middle of the night that the color of the table
napkins is wrong for tomorrow's party, is it just your brain going

into overdrive because you need approval from your social group because otherwise you will be left to die in the forest?

(v: Codependency, Control freaks, Safety)

❧

DATING

Always keep the door open. Love stories start every minute of the day: you never know what is around the corner. Keep shaking things up, breaking the rules and changing your habits. A recent scientific report suggests that by changing our routines we change our luck.

(v: Comfort zone, Complete wankers, Safety)

❧

DATING SITES

Ten years ago, people would rather have hung naked over a crocodile pit than admit they met through a lonely hearts ad. The very name screamed 'loser'. But now, thanks to cool online sites and classified ads, everyone has dabbled. Of course, it's lovely to meet in 'real life', where you can judge chemistry instantly. The fact that someone has walked across the room and chosen you is a great help. But over a certain age that room begins to get smaller. Sign up to a dating website and immediately you have more than 1,000 matches. You won't always fancy each other. But choice is everything. Don't spend too long e-flirting (it can be disappointing if you invest too much in the correspondence). After a couple of phone calls, arrange to meet. To be honest, the first time isn't a date. We can all be kind and convivial for an hour. Don't agree to a second date out of guilt, but be generous in your dismissal.

(v: Almost date, Dating, Good husband material)

DAUGHTERS

Daughters are one of life's great delights. It's lovely to have a Bonsai you. However, your daughter will need to separate from you at some point during adolescence and this can be a very painful process, not least because the warfare can be cruelly verbal as opposed to physical. Accept that this disconnection has to happen: pass the baton on, offer support and empathy but don't get in the way of your daughter's emerging independence.

(v: It's a girl, Mothers, Sisters, Sons)

DEALING NOT COPING

Women are very good at coping but sometimes the coping overwhelms the dealing. Problems become repetitive and, paradoxically, developing successful coping strategies can mean that you begin to take a much bigger share of responsibility while never resolving the underlying problems. The result is that you become exhausted, snappish, irritable and controlling. You feel exploited but can't quite explain why. So a home truth: many women complain endlessly about how much they have to do and how little time they have to do it, but won't let anybody else help. So don't be a martyr. Delegate what you can. Grasp the nettle and write down a list of things that are bothering you and take action.

(v: Big babies, Boundaries, Bullying, Codependency, Grasping the nettle)

DEBT

'Annual income twenty pounds, annual expenditure nineteen nineteen six, result happiness. Annual income twenty pounds, annual expenditure twenty pounds ought and six, result misery.'
– MR. MICAWBER, *DAVID COPPERFIELD*, CHARLES DICKENS

'All I ask is the chance to prove that money can't make me happy.'
– SPIKE MILLIGAN

'I'm living so far beyond my income we could be said to be living apart.'
– E. E. CUMMINGS

There is no excuse to be in debt, although probably most of us are in one way, shape or form. Take control. Buy an account book and work out your income and your outgoings. Then make the necessary cuts coalition style. It hurts, of course it does. But you'll get immense satisfaction from managing your money more effectively and once you cut unnecessary spending habits you'll begin to value the things you do spend money on, and enjoy planning for your future.

(v: Credit cards, Grasping the nettle, I can't afford to buy cheap, Money matters, Opening brown envelopes, Pensions)

DÉCOLLETAGE

Ooh la la. Ding dong. This is the coyest, sexiest part of your body and one you should know how to work and exploit, should you wish to do so. French women are all very good at protecting and projecting this area, but it needs daily attention. A combination of creams, massage and exercise will work well together but don't forget the vital element – the importance of posture. The overall aim is to have a dainty show of crêpe-free bosom, which you can expose with a certain amount of flirtation. If the male gaze is important to you, neglect your décolletage at your peril.

(v: Boobs)

DEFERMENT OF PLEASURE

It is a truth universally acknowledged that the survival of the human race has depended on the fact that women will defer their own pleasure for the sake of the greater good. In modern times we remain experts in this particular field and it's incredibly useful for all those not quite grown-up men around us that we do. Even the media, supposedly dominated by liberal types, absolutely consolidates this view. However, is there a slight whiff of martyrdom in all of this? Of course, it is good to meet your responsibilities: some would say that it is only by meeting them that we set ourselves free, but nowadays we seem to want to add even more great expectations to the mix. Can we only really let ourselves have a good time when we've stacked the dishwasher, lost ten pounds and recovered the lost ark of the covenant? Ten years later we might look back at a photograph and say: 'Heavens, I did have rather nice arms after all. I could have gone dancing and had fun and maybe got home a bit late and neither I nor the people I love would have been any the worse for it.'

(v: Orgasms)

<hr>

DEL CONTE, ANNA [ICON]
'There is nothing which bonds a family together more than a delicious meal enjoyed around a table. While you eat it conversations blossom, laughter explodes, discussions and arguments arise. In three short words: life becomes alive. There is nothing which expresses love more than good food, carefully and properly prepared, or at least that is what I hope since I have spent the best part of my adult life cooking and I have enjoyed every minute of it.'

(v: Cooking)

DEMONSTRATIONS
'I think you should take your job seriously, but not yourself.'
– JUDY DENCH

Please do go on these. You should not be deterred by scare-mongering newspapers. Terrible things are done in our name by politicians who we have voted into power. You have the right to protest about them. Just don't go around carrying a rock in your hand, or torturing policemen with poetry.

(v: Lipstick, Poetry)

DEPRESSION
'If you want the rainbow you gotta put up with the rain.'
– DOLLY PARTON

'In the midst of winter I found within myself an invincible summer . . .'
– ALBERT CAMUS

Depression is a generic term that covers a multitude of sins. For some people it's a phase, for others a spiritual event, or for the most unlucky it's a lifelong illness that has to be managed like any other chronic disease. Psychotherapists and psychiatrists are often at war when it comes to the treatment of depression, but don't be afraid to take medication despite the scaremongers. It can help enormously, if only to give you a break.

(v: Blues, Freud, Jung, Self-pity)

ယက

Detaching with love

A phrase that has eased itself into common parlance alongside the proliferation of Alcoholics Anonymous and other related self-help groups. In essence, it means that we can allow ourselves 'to love the person but not the disease', but that we do not have to, nor should we try to, engage with the emotional or practical carnage that often surrounds the addict. It is also a useful behavioral tool for daily life, actually you can detach with love from just about anybody who you feel is giving you a hard time. If this all sounds far too po-faced for its own good, be reassured, the phrase 'I'm detaching with love' can also be used to comic effect in a range of social situations, e.g. if you need to leave a party pronto, disengage from a bender or decide not to go to bed with a man you've recently snogged.

(v: Bad boys, Benders, Codependency, Dipsomania, Emergency exit)

ယက

Diamonds (are a girl's best friend)

Tradition suggests that a man should spend three months' salary on the engagement ring for his intended, and that nothing less than half a carat* will do. If there is a lovely man in the wings, this is the moment to fulfill your heart's desire. However, we all know that the path of true love doesn't always run smooth. Nowadays many a single gal buys her own ring, and all power to her elbow.

Make sure you buy the best diamonds you can afford. They come in all cuts and colors and are as hardy as hell, so don't just keep them for special occasions. Pink, to make the boys wink, is especially pretty. These sparklers will go with everything in your wardrobe and are a great investment, so bear that in mind too. Last but not least you can choose your stone then ask an à la carte jeweller to create something for you to your own design. How classy.

(v: Engagement)

* A carat is 0.20 grams.

⤫

Diets

'Never eat more than you can lift.'

– Miss Piggy

Yo-yo dieting is a feature of many women's lives but it can be bad for your health, and can, ironically, alter your natural metabolism, which makes it extremely hard to lose weight. What's important to understand and accept is your natural body shape, but what nobody wants to do is put on too much weight. Jill Shaw Ruddock rightly claims that we must concentrate on the noun rather than the verb.

(v: Ballooning weight, Carbohydrates, Cider vinegar,
Eat your greens, Trampolining)

⤫

Dignity

This may sound like a preposterous, perhaps old-fashioned, characteristic but it's rather like necessary vanity or secret confidence. It's a character-defining quality that can shape your life for the better. If you can manage not to lose your temper, whatever the slings and arrows of outrageous fortune, people will respect you for it. However, if you are holding your head up high while all around are losing theirs don't take the moral high ground. That just makes you a prig.

(v: Good behavior, Grace)

～

DILATION

CERVICAL

When you are having a baby your cervix needs to dilate to four inches. It's one of the rules. If it doesn't you will probably have to have a Caesarian. This will necessitate an epidural, which in the circumstances can be quite a relief.

PUPILS

If your pupils are dilating it may be to do with shock or pain or fabulous sex or it may be that you have taken too many recreational drugs. If the latter, it's a telltale sign easily spotted by canny teenagers and inquisitive bosses. Expensive sunglasses are helpful in these circumstances or you could just ease up on the hallucinogenics.

(v: Babies, Childbirth, Drugs, Sunglasses)

DIPSOMANIA

An old-fashioned word for alcoholism. There are very broad definitions of what makes an alcoholic and also very narrow ones but the governmental diktat to restrict yourself to a certain number of units a week is rather a blunt tool, which it seems the majority of regular drinkers find risible and routinely ignore. We are not natural killjoys but women are drinking more and more and for a variety of reasons it is no doubt injurious to our well-being. If you are worried about how much you are drinking, take a break. A little self-restraint from time to time is a good habit to acquire and one way forward is to abstain one day a week, one week a month and one month a year. Your health will benefit in all sorts of ways.

(v: Alcohol, Benders, Booty calls, Booze, Champagne, Cocktails,
Drunk-dialing, Emotional overdrinking)

DISHWASHERS

Many people spend more time loading and unloading the dishwasher than having sex.

This is unwise.

DIVORCE PARTIES

It may be that once the financial settlement has been agreed it's appropriate to crack open a bottle of champagne, but this may not be a triumphant gesture, rather a recognition that a long and usually agonizing process is now thankfully over. As for divorce parties, isn't that the equivalent of dressing head to toe in black crépe for a wedding?

(v: I don't, Lawyers)

DIY

Girls have solo sex too. *Sex and the City* blew the doors off with the episode that featured the Rampant Rabbit. No one needs to put up with bad behavior in a lover when you have all the resources you need for self-satisfaction. Plus there's some rather promising kit out there. Don't ever let anyone make you feel lonely or inadequate about having solo sex. Men have been feeling great about it for centuries.

(v: Le gadget)

Dogs

If you are newly single, or your children have just left home, or both, then maybe the time has come to think about getting a dog. It's a commitment. Like small children, they need a routine you can stick to, but in return they offer devoted companionship. They will also force you to exercise, a minimum of half an hour a day, and wherever you go you will make new friends. It's wise to get a '57 Varieties' mutt/mongrel (they won't suffer from congenital health problems in the way that some purebred dogs do). Do your research into the dog's provenance and its parents' sociability before going ahead, but look forward to a long friendship.

(v: Ballooning weight, Cats, Diets, Exercise, Waist)

ፀፚ

Don't!

'To tell a woman everything she may not do is to tell her the most she can do.'

– Spanish Proverb

ፀፚ

Don't sweat the small stuff

Unless life and limb are under threat, or human rights are being compromised, let it go. Life's far too short.

(v: It seemed like a good idea at the time, Regrets)

ፀፚ

Do tell!

Well, sometimes it is appropriate and sometimes it isn't. Generally information needs to be passed around, that is one of the functions and rewards of being part of a bigger society. However, if somebody asks you to keep their secret then you must do so and if somebody asks you to reveal somebody else's secret then you must resist. But we are all vulnerable to siren songs so don't beat your BFF up if she lets slip.

(v: BFF, Gossip, Secrets)

DOWN THE RABBIT HOLE

Sometimes in our overcontrolled and overplanned lives we need to just let things happen to us and the more chaotic, abstract and hallucinatory the better. If, like Alice, you find yourself falling down a rabbit hole, i.e. every intention and expectation you had about your life is being tested and everything you face is about to be transformed, succumb – in retrospect, the experience will be life-changing.

(v: Adventure)

DREAMS

'Be not afeard. The isle is full of noises,
Sounds and sweet airs that give delight and hurt not.
Sometimes a thousand twangling instruments
Will hum about mine ears, and sometimes voices
That, if I then had waked after a long sleep,
Will make me sleep again; and then, in dreaming,
The clouds methought would open, and show riches
Ready to drop upon me, that when I waked,
I cried to dream again.'

– *THE TEMPEST*, III. II., WILLIAM SHAKESPEARE

'We are such stuff
As dreams are made on; and our little life
Is rounded with a sleep.'
– *THE TEMPEST*, IV. I., WILLIAM SHAKESPEARE

'Dreams . . . they've gone through and through me,
like wine and through water, and altered the color of my mind.'
– *WUTHERING HEIGHTS*, EMILY BRONTË

'Dreaming is free.'
– 'DREAMING', DEBBIE HARRY

(v: Freud, Jung)

ↄↄ

DRUGS

Are as old as the hills. Folk the world over have been sniffng convivially and smoking and imbibing companionably since the golden age, obviously because by and large they are extremely enjoyable pursuits. Artists have always been attracted to substances that heighten feeling and produce altered states, as have shamans and religious visionaries. In the twenty-first century a gin and tonic and the occasional jazz cigarette or the like is not anyone else's business but yours and can be a good way of unwinding after a hard taxing day. Your body may well be a temple, or a Bedouin tent for all we know, but you are grown-up enough to make an informed decision. But all kinds of drugs including pharmaceuticals, and yes, boring old aspirin, tend to be addictive and their use needs monitoring so you do not get hooked.

If you have got teenagers and you come across any 'substances', you need to discuss them calmly and as soon as possible. The alternative is where addictions lie. Threatening hell and damnation will only make the kids go underground. You need to keep the debate ongoing and in the open. The bigger picture is that the illegal drugs industry is now worth trillions of dollars and brings criminality, destruction and death in its wake. But the genie is well and truly out of the bottle, whichever way you look at it. The case for proper education about, taxation and decriminalization of drugs has never looked stronger.

(v: Dilation, Drunk-dialling, Insomnia, Meds)

ᏉᏏᏜ

DRUNK-DIALING

You are, of course, over the affair. You are out with friends, it's a Friday, and you are boldly looking forward to the future, but after that third drink the small voice of doubt creeps in. Maybe it was my fault? Maybe I need to tell him how much I do love/hate him? Is he with somebody else? Is he missing me? It wouldn't do any harm to make the call. And so on and so forth . . . by closing time doubting Thomas has turned into a huge green glittering snake exhorting you to eat the apple. Before you know it, you are hitting speed dial. At this point your BFF will attempt to ascertain what is going on and then try to wrestle you to the floor, grab your phone and throw it in the nearest river – and not without reason, because she has spent every spare waking moment of the last three months listening sympathetically to your outpourings of rage and grief and the promise that you will never, ever speak to him again. But it's too late, the die is cast, you make the call. Even as you are doing it, you already know somewhere in your heart that when you wake up in the morning, whatever the outcome, you are going to absolutely hate yourself. There is only one solution: it's tough but mercifully simple. When an affair is over delete all phone and e-mail addresses from all relevant technology and keep it that way. He can always find you again if he wants to.

(v: Bad habits, Booty calls, Booze, Cocktails, Dipsomania)

DULLNESS

Is there any real excuse for dullness? There is surely little or no reason why people can't put effort into being amusing and entertaining company. A few anecdotes up your sleeve, some good jokes and a dash of piquant gossip are recommended. Be ready to be 'on'.

(v: Bores, Conversation)

EASE
'What if we just acted like everything was easy?'
– MARY ANNE RADMACHER

EAT YOUR GREENS

Mother was right: you should eat your greens. The importance of dark green vegetables in our diet is, quite simply, not to be trifled with. From decades of exhaustive research, by the men and women in white coats, we have the indisputable facts: folic acid and antioxidant-rich leafy vegetables can provide everything from a boost in your skin's radiance to a significant reduction in the risk of cancers and birth defects. We know that just three cups of fresh leaves a week can be invaluable to your health. If you find it all a bit goody two-shoes, the next time you are tucking into a bowl of salad greens consider the suggestion that you are eating sunshine. Sounds ridiculous but as any seven-year-old schoolkid will tell you, plants get their emerald hue from chlorophyll – a unique molecular structure, which allows them to capture and store the energy of sunlight. But whatever you wish to ponder as you chew, the main reason to eat green leaves is, of course, how they taste – elegant, complex and sophisticated. They look beautiful too. So toss them jauntily in a large bowl with a drizzling of balsamic, fresh lemon juice and extra-virgin olive oil and top them with all kinds of seeds and nuts, if you are so inclined. Divine.

(v: Ballooning weight, Climacteric, Diet)

ECCENTRICS
Fascinate and amusing with their slightly daffy differences and the way they stand out like a sore thumb in today's homogenized society. Bring them on, we say. Often geniuses or aristo-bohemians, they are usually preoccupied or obsessed with an idiosyncratic way of living, and have a tendency to strange garb and unusual habits. However, they often achieve wonders and are to be treasured accordingly. They make life much more funky.

ELDERLY PRIMAGRAVIDA
The average age for a woman to have her first baby in the United States has risen from 21 to 25 in the last thirty years. The term elderly primagravida is used to describe a woman of 35 years or

older who is expecting her first baby. Given that we are starting to have babies later and later, expect to hear this term more and more frequently – you may even be one yourself.

The pros of having a baby later are that you are far more likely to be calm and patient, and you won't worry about not going out to parties. However, it can be physically challenging and extremely exhausting.

(v: Babies, Childbirth, Fertility, Pregnancy)

ᴄ✍

ELEGANCE
'The only real elegance is in the mind;
if you've got that, the rest really comes from it.'
– DIANA VREELAND
(v: Beauty treatments, Camiknickers, Creative corsetry,
Exercise, Petticoats, Necessary vanity, Secret confidence)

ᴄ✍

E-MAIL XXING
Of course we don't really LOVE them. But the screen 'X' is women's secret weapon: a way to lighten up a bossy e-mail to a coworker, or shorthand for 'we're still cool' after a slightly tricky missive. A couple of hundred years ago, it might have been an open sexual invitation. Now it's just a nice, platonic way of saying, 'Thanks for fixing the photocopier'.

(v: Technology, XXXs)

EMERGENCY EXIT

Whether you are simply at a ghastly party, at the back of a disorderly queue or floundering in a relationship that is making you extremely unhappy, don't be afraid to use the emergency exit. That's what it's there for.

(v: Crisis, Leaving the party)

EMOTIONAL OVERDRINKING

Yes, alcohol is the symptom but it's the self-hatred the next day that is ruining our lives. We wake up hungover, our body flooded with stress chemicals, which, apart from anything else, affect our metabolism.

Try to have at least one alcohol-free day a week. Avoid friends who are simply looking for a drinking partner. There are ways of resisting peer pressure with little white lies, such as 'I'm on antibiotics' or 'I've got a hangover from last night'.

Instead of pouring that glass, pamper yourself in different ways, e.g. a long aromatherapy bath, a massage or that DVD you've been meaning to watch.

(v: Alcohol, Booty calls, Cocktails, Dipsomania, Drunk-dialing, Wine)

ENGAGEMENT

People make a fuss of you when you get engaged and so they should. Enjoy every last minute.

(v: Catching the bouquet, Hen nights, Wearing white dresses)

⮑

ENIGMA

It's hard to remain an enigma when we live in a world where everybody is intent on revealing every little thing about themselves at parties and then revealing it again on Facebook. But do try it. If in doubt, cast your mind back to *Brief Encounter* and imagine how the whole caboodle would have been blown out of the water if Celia Johnson had received a text at the wrong minute. Being enigmatic is a very sexy quality indeed.

(v: Instinct, Power, Sense of self)

⮑

ENTERING A CONVENT

Who hasn't had that fleeting moment while watching Julie Andrews in *The Sound of Music* when you think, 'Surely I'd look great in a wimple?'

Before the emancipation of women 'becoming a bride of Christ' was a career opportunity. It meant that one could escape an arranged marriage and the attendant risks of childbirth and have some hope of a rudimentary education. Historically, women of a certain class could seek refuge in a convent, sometimes because of political necessity, cf. Eleanor of Aquitaine, or simply because they wanted to withdraw from a secular life.

Nowadays to become a nun one must be Catholic, female, unmarried and sane. Women who are not virgins can become nuns (this is a big breakthrough) but Roman Catholic women who are divorced may not generally become nuns unless they have received an annulment from the Catholic Church. They must prove that the marriage was somehow invalid or contracted under false pretenses in order for an annulment to be granted.

A widowed woman may become a nun, but generally she must have raised any children to the age of 18 prior to taking vows, since these vows would supersede the care of her own children.

Some nuns are religious scholars, and sometimes it may be necessary to have a college education prior to joining an order. Twenty-first century nuns can work as nurses, teachers, doctors or psychologists and often play an active role in the service of their local communities. So, if you're a dab hand at running up dirndl skirts made out of damask curtains this may be the job for you.

(v: Chastity)

∽

EROTICA

'Pornography is about dominance and often pain.
Erotica is about mutuality and always pleasure.'
– GLORIA STEINEM

Desire begins in the head for many of us and women are just as entitled to visual stimuli as men. It may be looking at sensual photographs, buying rock star underwear or a visit to a burlesque club, but erotica is about falling in love with yourself a little: giving yourself permission to act out private fantasies – alone, or with a significant other. Erotica shapes our life in a very important way. It adds texture and spice to life. Don't let go of that just because you hate porn.

(v: Creative corsetry, pornography)

∽

(THE) EX (PLURAL)

Oh the ex. The ex is only really the ex when you simply don't fancy him anymore. Of course, he probably won't ever believe that to be the case and he will fondly (or otherwise) imagine that you will carry a torch for him until your dying day. But now he has run off with the au pair, someone else can do your dirty work, and gradually the love and agony you feel will turn to anger and hatred and probably end up as ambivalence. If, however, the very sound of his dulcet tones has you running for the vodka bottle, just steady yourself, make a written note of the things you wish to relay to him pertaining to the children in words of no more than two syllables and sentences of no more than ten words. Then have a stiff one.

(v: Agony, Divorce)

∽

EXERCISE
(v: Arms, Boxing, Comfort zone, Cycling, Pilates, Tap dancing, Trampolining, Yoga)

EXPANDING UNIVERSE

Try different music you haven't heard before. Tune into a different radio station. Learn another language. Try new foods. Mix things up sometimes just to get a fresh perspective. It could be as simple as moving the furniture or sleeping on the other side of the bed.

Push the limits of your body by taking up martial arts. Learn to do a handstand. Try meditation or open your mind to other political or religious points of view. Even if you don't agree, you'll be able to argue much more intelligently.

People report that learning a new thing every day makes them happier than sex. Whatever you learn encourages new neural pathways in the brain and, over time, with repetition, you gradually become better at something. The human brain is infinite, we use about an eighth of it. You can keep learning until the day you die. Queen Elizabeth II has made it a lifelong habit to learn a new fact every day.

(v: Comfort zone, Handstand revolution)

EXPENSIVE

You will always treasure something lovely and probably ridiculously expensive, whether it's a diving watch, a loud-print Italian dress or a delicious and fragrant face cream and make really good use of it because you have invested in it and for very good reasons. It is probably beautiful, well made and of exceptional quality. Wearing or using it can often make you feel like a million dollars, which is just as well.

(v: I can't afford to buy cheap)

❧

EXTENDED FAMILIES

In fluid and/or 'blended' families, the general feeling is, the more the merrier. So park any annoying, grinding irritations that you have with your in-laws and your daughter's puerile boyfriend or ex-husband's trophy wife, and swiftly opt for the 'killing with kindness' policy. Where children and elderly parents are concerned, put aside your differences, there is no point in making other people's lives miserable because you can't sort out your own. Life, as they say, is far too short and you will feel quite angelic to boot. The children will love to see everyone getting on and, as a proper grown-up, you owe it to them to make that happen.

(v: The Ex, I don't, In-laws, Teenagers, Stepchildren)

❧

EYES

The windows to the soul and our greatest natural asset. Eyes matter: for communicating, bartering, flirting. They speak even when you are silent. In the twenty-first century, well-shaped eyebrows can open up the face and take ten years off us and false eyelashes are no longer the preserve of drag queens.

(v: Dilation)

Facial exercises

There is a growing realization that what is under your skin is as important as what goes on it. The 'working out' of facial muscles keeps them toned. They are the 'coat hanger' your face fits on. If you see somebody at the traffic lights involved in a curious kind of gurning and stretching of their face, they may be doing the work required to keep themselves looking lovely. This includes stretching the distance between lid and brow, forehead, lifting cheek and jowl muscles, and working the neck area to avoid extra padding. For those who want serious and natural results, these steps are the key and, once you've learned them, they are yours for life. A little bit of face toning won't go amiss either.

(v: Blow jobs, Good stuff that's free)

৩৯৯

FALSE EYELASHES

Invented by D. W. Griffths in 1916 for the heroine of his epic movie *Intolerance*. Stars such as Dietrich, Hayworth and Lamarr understood that a languorous close-up could be stronger than a thousand pictures. Post the sixties, false eyelashes went into decline and became largely the province of transvestites, but in the last couple of years there has been a 'falsie' revival. Now everyone is experimenting with extensions, lash-regenerating mascara and magic regrowth formulas that are applied nightly.

Michelle Obama wears false lashes. Lady Gaga sports feathered lash sets. Shu Uemura has made custom-designed mink lashes with diamonds for Madonna. Long eyelashes are associated with youthfulness, lashes get shorter as you grow older and hormone levels change, and glossy eyelashes are signs of health and fertility and raw sex appeal.

Falsies are a great way to change your look without having to do something invasive. You can choose from one or two spider's legs added to the edge of the eye to enhance a sexy flutter, or go for the full caterpillar effect.

Lash extensions $100–$150 are more costly but last up to three months if you have top-ups. All you need to do is comb them in the mornings.

(v: Necessary vanity)

~~~

FAMILY

'Happy families are all alike; every unhappy family
is unhappy in its own way.'
– *ANNA KARENINA*, LEO TOLSTOY

They drive you mad, push your buttons and no one knows better how to get under your skin than a member of your family. But it's the only one you get. We all have a vision of how we'd like family life to be, but we may have to let go of those fantasies. While a shared past can be a bond, we also know rather too much about each other.

Birth order, age difference and gender may also give us different perceptions of the same childhood experiences – differences that can be hard to reconcile.

No family is the same. For some raised voices could be traumatic; for others this could be the usual form of communication. If all parties are willing to hang in there and change direction when they make mistakes, the relationship can be rescued.

If you're dealing with a silly spat that can be resolved informally, take the plunge and phone. Better to sort out a problem before it becomes a major hemorrhage.

Treat each other with the courtesy and respect that you would extend to friends and colleagues. If necessary lie politely. Then go home and have a very large gin and tonic.

(v: Brothers, Daddy damage, Daughters, Family therapy,
Mothers, Sisters, Sons, Teenagers)

⁓

FAMILY THERAPY
Can be agonizing, but also surprisingly helpful.

(v: Brothers, Daddy damage, Daughters, Mothers,
Sisters, Sons, Teenagers)

⁓

FASTING

Biblical in many senses, fasting is worth doing to blast your system. Most people eat way too much so, once in a while, warm water and lemon for a day or two is to be embraced. You feel very worthy afterwards, which is why so many religions encourage it: it helps cleanse the system, reboots your metabolism and can give you a slightly heady weightless feeling, which may make you susceptible to heavenly visions. However, don't try to fast if you are pregnant, have a chronic or life-threatening illness, have a busy working day or you are breast-feeding. It's not fair on anybody, least of all yourself.

(v: Cider vinegar, Diets)

⁓

FEAR
'All that ever holds somebody back, I think, is fear.
For a minute I had fear. [Then] I went into the [dressing] room
and shot my fear in the face . . .'
– LADY GAGA

FEET

Never begrudge spending money on your feet. It's not just girlish vanity. Feet are the foundation of the body. Feet keep you standing upright. A foot can sustain enormous pressure, several tons over the course of a one-mile run, and provide flexibility and resiliency. There are 26 bones (one-quarter of the bones in the human body are in the feet), 33 joints and over 100 muscles, tendons and ligaments in each foot.

And there's no need to be ashamed of your feet. A good chiropodist or podiatrist can rescue the worst corns and calluses – and often give you back the feet of a child! We're not just talking a colorful toe varnish, a medi-pedicure is as important as visiting the dentist. Bad foot care is akin to poor oral hygiene.

First your therapist will use a scalpel, lancet or drill to eliminate corns, calluses or thickening layers of skin (you will feel nothing, it's all dead). Next they will file and reshape the nail – straight, not too short to avoid ingrown nails. Then during a lower leg and foot massage, each muscle, tendon and joint is manipulated to liberate the bones. Women who wear high shoes need to keep their feet mobile. Podiatrists see women of 35 and over who can no longer put their back heel on the floor. Invest in regular massage to prevent you from having the joints of an 85-year-old.

Please, please, please look after your feet. They deserve to be treated with respect.

(v: Flats, Orthopedic footwear)

ოთა

FEMALE COMEDIANS

A great female comedian is like an unexploded bomb in a handbag. She might go off at any minute – voicing extreme rage – or she might apply her lipstick and play nice. From Tina Fey to Amy Sedaris and Chelsea Handler, the best writer-performers find a way to say the unsayable. From cancer to suicide and disability, no subject is too sacred. Women and gay men – who routinely see themselves caricatured on TV – respond to the raw power, the amorality of the great female comedy performer. They make us howl, they make us blush ('I can't possibly admit that I do that'), they make us rightly furious. But dear God they make us feel better about ourselves.

ოთა

FEMALE FOE

There is a particular type of single white female who, while pretending to want to be your best friend, actually wants to take on your life. She may start by copying your clothes, then the way you laugh, she may adopt your friends and/or your parents and turn up for Christmas and expect a stocking. She will probably end up by stealing your man. It can seem quite flattering to begin with but behind the scenes she is already reading your diary in secret and thieving small possessions, such as lipsticks and silk stockings. This can become a form of psychological torment. So beware of the signs, confront her immediately and send her on her way.

(v: Frenemies, Mistress, Well put together)

 භ

FERTILITY

The received wisdom is that in one's teens and twenties one is ridiculously fertile, but this lessens once we hit our mid-thirties and if you haven't had a baby by the time you are forty you may face some challenges if you want to get pregnant. However, everybody has a story to prove the opposite and it is also clear that some couples can get more easily pregnant than others. Sadly infertility, despite all the advances in health and well-being, has become something of an epidemic in the Western world and hand in hand with that epidemic a major medical industry has evolved. Older male gynecologists tell us that we are just leaving it too late and that by selfishly pursuing a career we only have ourselves to blame if we can't get pregnant. The more enlightened baby doctors will recommend some form of medical intervention if we don't get pregnant within a certain time frame. Poor diet, stress, lack of exercise and PVC packaging are all cited as additional reasons for infertility and so people trying to get pregnant can find themselves in a very stressful cycle of self-improvement, often driven by very conflicting advice, as they try to create the perfect body environment for conception. Our suggestion is Five Element acupuncture, but if the clock is ticking seek medical advice.

(v: Contraception, Elderly primagravida, Five Element acupuncture, Magic spells, Pregnancy)

༄

FILM CLUB (START A)

Finding it diffcult to drag someone along to see the latest Almodóvar? Prefer documentaries to blockbusters? Then start a film club. *Ciné-clubs* were originally set up in Paris in the 1920s to bring film lovers together in an informal situation to watch screenings that were hard to see in mainstream cinemas. There was usually delicious food and drink on hand too.

You can take turns hosting a film club. All you need is a decent DVD player, or a projector and a white wall. Alternatively, look out for hotels and independent cinemas with their own film clubs: they will often include lunch or supper as part of the event. It doesn't have to be a room full of earnest filmmakers in black polo necks. There are sci-fi film clubs, foreign film festivals, screwball comedy and eighties nostalgia nights.

Film is a brilliant way to connect with new people. In contrast to stilted conversation at parties or private viewings, there's a brief initial chat over a glass of wine and then you get to sit in the dark for two long hours – and wallow. After the screening everyone is so fired up that the evening flows freely. You are bound to meet like-minded people sooner rather than later, and whether you find a lover or discover your new best friend, you know that you share a mutual passion.

༄

FINANCES

(v: Frightening bank managers, Money matters, Pensions,
Something for a rainy day)

↭

F IS FOR FUNNY

'You can't really be strong until you can see a funny side to things.'
– *ONE FLEW OVER THE CUCKOO'S NEST*, KEN KESEY

And 'funny' puts the wind in your sail, the cream in your coffee and the screw in your screwball. If you can be around funny people and folk with fizz, your life will be impeccably leavened forever. The chintz may be sagging, a higgledy-piggledy state may reign slightly more than it ought to on the domestic front, but hey, if someone or something can stick a smile on your face then everyone is singing for their supper.

↭

FIRES

If you are lucky enough to have a fireplace, lighting a fire in the family hearth is one of life's great pleasures and is one of the few upsides of the arrival of November and the start of a long winter. A fire brings warmth and the natural element of wood into the home. And in the depths of a bleak mid-winter it can bring soul, coziness and good cheer. Summer fires, lit late at night with the windows open against the backdrop of a velvety blue sky, have their own strange beauty and outside fires or fire pits can bring a pagan grandeur to any occasion. If you live near the sea and can collect driftwood it will add the sulphurous colors of blue and green to the flames.

Some people are instinctive fire makers – although there is no rhyme or reason to this – but, if in doubt, do keep a stash of matches handy and use them liberally.

(v: Candles, Magic spells)

◊

FISHING FOR COMPLIMENTS
We prefer deep-sea diving.

◊

FITTING IN
Nobody loves pedantic, fussy, demanding women and there is nothing more aging. Go with the flow. It's what makes the world go around.

(v: Flow, Old ladyish behavior, Satisficers)

◊

FIVE ELEMENT ACUPUNCTURE
Originally based on the Tao, Five Element acupuncture was a preventative system of medicine favored by the 'princes' of Ancient China. By balancing the body's Five Elements, boosting the immune system and ensuring the free-flow of 'chi' or life-energy, the healer would also treat each individual in relation to his or her community. In the twenty-first century medical experts have found little proof through scientific study of its efficaciousness and remain sceptical of its healing powers, even though hundreds and thousands of westerners, who visit

acupuncturists on a regular basis, swear by it. So how do we bridge this contradiction? It seems unlikely that acupuncture is the cure for chronic illness but it is also possible that the very physical connection between acupuncturist and patient and the time that the practitioner spends with a patient has a life-enhancing effect. If you feel well, you are well. If you are finding that more conventional forms of medicine and therapy are not doing the trick it may well be worth giving it a go – particularly for depression, fertility problems, insomnia and low libido.

(v: Botox, Facial acupuncture, Fertility)

FLATS

Oh the deep, deep peace of flat shoes after the true agony of bone-bending stilettos, cf. *The Little Mermaid.* Occasionally it really is worth giving up on 'girl' shoes. You'll save a small fortune on plasters and blister dressings. Men will respect your speed and dexterity (if, indeed, you care about their good opinion of you) and you'll lose weight (because you can walk further). Plus flats don't have to be dull – think handmade brogues, ballet pumps, roll up real cotton ballet shoes in your handbag just in case, delicate flip-flops, silver sneakers or kick-ass biker boots.

(v: Feet, High heels)

⤫

FLIRTATION

It's all in the eyes, so take off your sunglasses. Be very interested, even if you are not.

(v: Sunglasses, Trysts)

⤫

FLOW

All of us know that wonderful feeling of being so caught up in something that we stop watching the clock. It's particularly important to experience this in the busy lives that we lead. Positive psychologists call it 'flow'. Virtually anything can be a flow activity – reading, telling a story, ice skating, painting, singing in a choir and even socializing.

You will know if you have had a 'flow experience' because you will become immersed in whatever you are doing and remember it afterwards as highly gratifying and fulfilling. Scientists say it raises our level of happiness because we are most 'ourselves' when we are caught up in the moment and when we are able to forget temporarily the daily grind: bad hair days, irritating in-laws, tax bills.

The trick is to identify our key flow activity – the thing that gives us most pleasure – and factor more of it into our lives.

(v: Choirs, Reading groups, Yoga)

ᘓᙥ

FLOWERS

A woman carrying flowers always looks gorgeous – it implies an admirer has just sent you a bouquet, or that you are taking them to a friend, which means that you are a wonderful and generous human being. But whatever and whoever they are for, they will make you happy. Buy yourself a bunch of flowers, however small, once a week and put them by your bed. If your budget is tight, and the onset of autumn is making you feel gloomy, invest in some basic terracotta pots and bulbs: plant crocuses, hyacinths and daffs in October in pots and keep in a dark cool place. They will flower about Christmastime and will keep you going through winter and into spring. A vase of dead flowers can also look rather spectacular in its own kind of way, but don't go too Miss Havisham.

(v: Catching the bouquet, Container gardens)

ᘓᙥ

FOOD

(v: Anna Del Conte, Carbohydrates, Cooking, Gelati,
Old-fashioned Italian restaurants)

ᘓᙥ

FRANKNESS

Political correctness has somewhat muddied the waters around lasses simply being able to speak their mind, which is something of a shame as treading on eggshells is so dull. As long as you are not planning to scare the horses, being clear about your feelings and saying what you think is a way of being true to yourself, although it may be best to hold back where the boss or mother-in-law is concerned.

(v: Anger)

പ

FREELANCE
(v: Portfolio careers)

പ

FRENEMIES

'Always forgive your enemies; nothing annoys them so much.'
– OSCAR WILDE

'Keep your friends close and your enemies closer.'
– MICHAEL CORLEONE IN *THE GODFATHER: PART II*

Occasionally there are people in your life who you liked once but for some reason, often lost in the mists of time, you like no longer. You still see them about, you are still reasonably friendly toward them when face to face, but secretly your inner dog doesn't like their inner dog very much. However, at some unconscious level you are unable to detach from them completely. Our view, which may feel initially unpopular, is to stay with your frenemies. There is probably an undiscovered reason why you still feel connected to them at some level, and while you work out what that is it's probably better having them inside the tent than not.

(v: Female foe, Persephone, Schadenfreude)

∼

FREUD

When in doubt, read Freud. From dreams and errors to jokes and symptoms, the father of psychoanalysis is never dull, although in many areas discredited. Like the Victorian gentleman he was, he believed women should be sweet domestic creatures, but he was one of the first to acknowledge women had sexual desire, and that repression of that sexual desire could make us supremely lonely or hysterical (just like men). He also made us sound bloody interesting, declaring, 'The great question that has never been answered, and which I have not yet been able to answer, despite my thirty years of research into the feminine soul, is "What does a woman want?"' To be honest we're still puzzling that one out ourselves. But it's nice when someone asks. For that alone we can forgive him penis envy.

(v: Depression, Dreams, Jung)

∼

FRIENDS
(v: Aloneness, BFF, Frenemies, Schadenfreude)

❧

FRIGHTENING BANK MANAGERS

They don't really exist nowadays because so much banking is done on the Internet. If you need a loan, an emergency overdraft, a mortgage, a pension or advice for what to do with a small nest egg, you will be put through to the relevant department and advised accordingly. However, if you are summoned to the bank to be grilled by the powers that be, always wear a suit and carry a broadsheet newspaper or a copy of *Liar's Poker* by Michael Lewis (a riveting and terrifying account of what banks do with your money, even if you haven't got any). You will be taken much more seriously.

(v: Debt, Money matters, Pensions, Something for a rainy day)

❧

FROCKS

From little black dresses and shirtwaisters to Diane von Furstenberg's forgiving wrap dresses, it's all about the frock. One-piece dressing is practical – you don't have to coordinate a frock with anything else, saving time in the morning. A dress will take you from day to evening (for posh, simply add a necklace and heels). Coat dresses are even better if you are forgetful, or just can't bear carrying stuff to parties or the theater.

But it's the 'frockness' of the frock that needs celebrating. Nothing skims curves more kindly than a dress: it can give you a nipped-in waist and a hint of cleavage and exudes grown-up femininity. If you tend to be a jeans girl or are simply addicted to casual dressing, the power of putting on a frock once in a while cannot be overstated. People melt.

The trick is to find your best shape. The silhouette matters. Apples suit tailored shifts; those with a *Mad Men* va-va-voom figure are best with 1950's styles; long lean types can go shorter than they think, especially with opaque tights, God's own gift to women.

Make sure you go for a lined frock (no wrinkles) that allows you to bend, reach, etc. without embarrassment or the loud splitting of seams. The rule of thumb is low neckline or lots of leg, but not both: no one wants to be mutton dressed as a vamp. Remember, sleeves can cover a multitude of sins, so add a lace cardigan or shrug to a sleeveless shift. Pockets tend to divide the fashionistas: yes, they slightly spoil the line, but heavens, women need secret spaces for lipstick, credit cards, etc. A great fabric is like a walking painting. Don't underestimate the power of color – it can be too easy to stay in black. A low-cut back or asymmetric sleeve adds amusement. You don't have to be traditionally girlie: Coco Chanel's exquisite navy-and-white shift dresses took their inspiration from nuns' habits and military uniforms.

Hemlines are a barometer of social and economic change. Dior brought in the New Look after the Second World War. The return of luxurious fabrics after rationing revolutionized the figure. Conversely, Mary Quant's sixties mini tunics were designed to allow women (normally trussed up in suits and pearls) to be able to run and skip, just like small children.

Dresses allow you to play out discreet fantasies – who am I today? Businesswoman or femme fatale? Sometimes it's fun to be restrained and ladylike. At other times you want a great no-fuss summer dress that reminds you of your teenage self. There's one for every mood and for every social encounter. Also, frocks are very helpful for dates with carnal conclusions (easy to take off without fumbling). And remember, men love buttons (don't even question it). But actually, frocks are for women. Frock envy is what makes the world go around. So please don't wait until you lose three stone. Every girl deserves a great dress.

(v: Bombshell, Color, Pears, Shapes, Waist)

Fruit

Many of us struggle to make our five a day but snacking on fruit can give you a fantastic boost. Berries are best and accompanied by cream make the most delicious and easy puddings ever invented.

(v: Blueberries, Cooking, Diets, Eat your greens, Hospitality)

Funerals

Always write a letter of condolence first. Try not to cry so much that you draw attention to yourself, which can be very embarrassing unless, of course, you are a professional mourner and get paid to do so. And, if you feel it's all going to be too much, there is nothing to stop you having a brandy with a friend before the event. Make sure you have a good hanky or two, your outfit is smart, leave plenty of time to get to your destination and make sure you know exactly where it is. Be very sensitive with the immediate family, and follow the general flow with the seating in church, i.e. do not squish yourself into the front row. Think it through. Remembering something funny, loving or meaningful about the deceased to tell their family and friends at the wake can be helpful and cheering. Take some flats in case it turns into a party.

(v: Grief, Leaving the party)

FUR

'All fur coat and no knickers' is a slight aimed at a so-called 'common' gal. It implies louche morals and general all-round bawdiness. But who can deny the touch of glamour derived by the hint of the mink or a wrap of raccoon? Of course, you need to bear in mind that these beautiful and fetching items have been borderline non-PC for several decades, but as long as the pieces you are wearing are vintage and have been dead as a doornail for quite some time it is silly not to do them the honor of wearing them. Toasty warm, heart-stoppingly sexy, throwing on a fur is a quick way to add some old school pizzazz to your outfit. And, for what it's worth, the heart of a caveman beats in most blokes, they are suckers for a fox in a fur.

(v: Animal prints, Caveman moment)

GALLERIES

Keep your visual stimuli high. You don't always have to do a three-hour blockbuster exhibition. Get into the habit of dropping into smaller galleries or museums. Revisit a favorite painting on your lunch hour, go around with an audio guide or ask the gallery attendant at least one question that will shed new light on your favorite artist. Alternatively, take a day off and embark on a galleryathon. Reading artists' biographies can give you a richer understanding of their goals and, yes, love lives. Don't worry that you have to understand art intellectually before you can appreciate it. Your immediate response and own interpretation is the cornerstone to developing a critical sensibility. Maybe the piece will awaken a long-forgotten memory or a strong emotional feeling will wash over you. Whatever happens, it's all good. You might even become inspired to try something new when you leave, cf. Tracey Emin's bed, and don't feel guilty just dropping in to use the café or shop. Anything that inspires the gallery habit is legitimate!

∾

GAP YEAR

Everyone is doing it and it's not necessarily poverty theme park tourism. Why not rent out your home for a few months and pad off with a partner or friend to one or two places where you have always wanted to go? You don't have to be in search of anything except the spirit of adventure, the chance to learn new skills and maybe the opportunity to share yours around. Those with teaching degrees can go forth and earn a living almost anywhere, the possibilities are endless. However, resist the temptation to sell property to fund a year out. It's a dangerous move. After all, you need to be able to come home in due course.

(v: Adventure)

∾

GARDENS
(v: Container gardens)

∾

GARTERS AND STOCKINGS
(v: Affairs, Cinq à sept, Have you got the kit?, Twice is polite)

ल्ल

GAY BEST FRIENDS

Gay friends are a joy. But they are your friends first and foremost – and gay second. No one goes out hiring based on sexuality. These days it's all about blended friendships. The term 'fag hag' is an affront. And – let's get this straight – gay and lesbian friends are not automatically any better at interior design, shopping or cushion plumping than anyone else. They're just as likely to be mad about football or *Top Gear* and they may also be married with children.

What GBFs are good at is pleasure. Our younger trailblazing GBFs get there first on every trend – from nightclubs and lectures to great venues for birthday parties. Just check out their Facebook sites for their latest downloads. Their judgement is impeccable – and they have the best address books. They don't blanch about going to expensive restaurants or paying for taxis.

If you're not part of the 1.8 nuclear family, GBFs can prove to be a gift from God over Christmas. They will offer open house with a five-course lunch, champagne and karaoke. You can bring a mother or two (if she behaves), but it's quite clear who's in charge.

Lesbian and gay friends tend to be sexually liberal and politically informed and they certainly won't let you become complacently liberal. Homophobic bullying remains a hot issue for gay men and women. They'll sharpen up your wardrobe and give great relationship advice. But you have to earn their friendship. GBFs can see through the smug marrieds who just want a godparent for their offspring.

If a gay power couple splits, your loyalties can truly be torn. Unlike many straight couples, you tend to like them both equally. But after the initial grief of parting, ex-gay partners often end up friends, they may even go on holiday together with their new lovers. It's all so bloody civilized. Clearly we heterosexuals have a lot to learn.

(v: Cocktails, Cross-generational friendship, Escaping your comfort zone, Imaginary love affairs with gay best friends)

GELATI

The ultimate girl food. Gelati – Italian ice cream – has a smooth texture with a burst of intense flavor and is amazingly low in fat (less than half the fat of traditional ice cream). Forget boring old vanilla or raspberry ripple, these days flavors include pine nut and fennel seed, hazelnut meringue, pumpkin, mascarpone or apple and cinnamon, alongside versions of Italian classics such as pistachio, *stracciatella* and dark chocolate. Sometimes it's a relief to skip the main course and head straight for the dessert bar. And you can always top up with a little brandy. It goes down a treat.

(v: Little bit of what you fancy does you good)

✍

GET OUT OF A RUT AND GET INVOLVED

The two go hand in hand. There's no better way to blow off the cobwebs, to recover from the end of a relationship or seize the moment than by getting involved with other people.

(v: Bouncing back, Canceling Christmas, Choirs, Churches, Film club, Gap year)

✍

GETTING INTO A FIGHT

'First they ignore you. Then they laugh at you. Then they fight you. Then you win.' – MAHATAMA GHANDI

✍

GIGOLO

The true gigolo isn't out to humiliate women. He's only passing through. No doubt he'll end up with someone younger or older than you but for a summer, he's yours. And that might be worth picking up the tab for. For women there is more equality in this relationship than you might think, and a healthy dose of realism. Seasoned women get company, emotional support and – sometimes – sex. And there's a lot that a gigolo can learn from their Mrs. Robinson.

✍

GIRL CRUSH

It could be your boss, or Alison Goldfrapp, or that fascinating woman at the library. It's like a mini love affair. You quote her all the time, start watching the DVDs she recommends, and wonder out loud if it's 'too soon' to ring her. You both want to be her, and be her best friend. Usually nonsexual in nature – sorry boys – but no less thrilling.

(v: Baby dykes)

GLOVES

'A lady is known by her shoes and her gloves.'
– *MRS. DALLOWAY*, VIRGINIA WOOLF

The opening chapter of *Mrs. Dalloway* – as Clarissa searches for the perfect white gloves, 'above the elbow', with pearl buttons – packs the punch of an emotional thriller.

But then gloves, from bejewelled lace to buttoned kid, have always been about seduction. Gloves embody practical elegance. And to be damn practical about it, they keep you warm and stop the spread of germs. They are also a brilliant punctuation point: if you need a moment to impress, or slow conversation down, there's something rather thrilling about watching a woman take off her gloves, finger by seductive finger, cf. *The Age of Innocence.*

GLUTEN-FREE

Life's too short.
(v: Carbohydrates)

∽

GODMOTHERS

Let's be frank about this. Godparents have little to do with God, or in fact parents. Godchildren are essentially the love child of a friendship born in your twenties or thirties (sometimes even further back) and it can be a relationship that struggles to survive the trials and tribulations of their divorce, or yours. If you ask a cross section of disgruntled teens 'What have your godparents done for you lately?' The answer is probably, 'Not enough'.

That is not to say that there aren't masses of kids with cases of port maturing slowly in order to be cracked open on an eighteenth birthday and guzzled by a group of motley Facebook friends, but on the whole, godparents are a slack lot, often very self-absorbed and once they have their own kids even less interested in their godparenting duties.

So if you are a godmother, focus on your inner 'fairy'. If you are not good at remembering birthdays, stow away the odd bit of cash in a post office account. (Godparents are duty-bound to give small but meaningful amounts of money to godchildren at odd times.) However, the occasional lovely lunch or a trip to the theater can be a real treat for your godchildren too. A letter at important moments in their lives, a phone call, a postcard from abroad, all show you've thought of them. And the thought really does count.

(v: BFF, Technology, Teenagers)

༚

GOING TO PRISON

Probably the best lie-down you can have on the cheap. A chance to catch up on your reading, learn to garden, keep down your phone bills, and somebody else cooks Christmas dinner. You can look forward to your freedom party too.

(v: Bolt-hole, Infinite vistas)

༚

GOOD BEHAVIOR

One of life's great protective mechanisms.
(v: Courtesy, Dignity, Grace, Punctuality)

༚

GOOD HUSBAND MATERIAL

'Chains do not hold a marriage together. It is thread, hundreds of tiny threads which sew people together.'
– SIMONE SIGNORET

'Only choose in marriage a man whom you would choose as a friend if he were a woman.'
– JOSEPH JOUBERT

A good man is hard to find but not impossible.

As Gloria Steinem wryly notes, we are becoming the men we wanted to marry. Assured, self-reliant, economically independent, sexually liberal, with a credit card and (hopefully) a rather nice apartment.

This fact is often used as a stick to beat single gals – cue the hilarious joke: 'Single women over the age of 35 are more likely to be killed by a terrorist than get married.' But, you know, it's a good thing. We don't need a husband to do the DIY/fix the car/deal with the bank. We can either do those things ourselves or pay someone else to do them. Just as men don't need a little woman to cook, clean and home-make. It's all up for grabs.

What we do want in good husband material is kindness, respect, adventurousness, curiosity – and a dynamo in the bedroom. A keeper, basically.

(v: A good man is hard to find, Dating, I don't, Top table)

෨ෆ

GOOD STUFF THAT'S FREE
(v: Churches, Galleries, Libraries, Parks, Seaside)

෨ෆ

GOOGLING YOURSELF
This has a peculiar and vaguely masturbatory quality about it. Try it once, but from then on it should be avoided at all costs unless you wish to go truly barmy.

෨ෆ

GOSSIP
(v: Small talk)

༕

GRACE

'Happy is your Grace,
That can translate the stubbornness of fortune
Into so quiet and so sweet a style.'
– *As You Like It*, II. i., WILLIAM SHAKESPEARE

We all have a higher self somewhere inside us. This is where your capacity for kindness, wisdom and courtesy meets your love of family and your generosity toward your friends and workmates transcends any negative or bad feelings you have had. Graciousness reigns in this realm and if you can access your higher self in times of strife it may well get you out of all kinds of trouble and bring with it a feeling of great calm and serenity.

(v: Dignity, Good behavior, Old-fashioned Italian restaurants)

༕

GRANDPARENTS

Be extremely nice to your children's grandparents, give them the keys to your house, and ask them to help with your babies. Their goodwill must never be abused.

(v: Babies, Divorce, Family therapy, Extended family, In-laws)

༕

GRAPPA

The grown-up *digestif* of choice. You only need a slug to experience the heat, kick and high alcohol content (between

40% and 60% by volume). Made from the leavings of the grapes after winemaking, grappa is primarily served as an after-dinner drink to aid the digestion of heavy meals. The fine versions come in beautiful hand-blown bottles, but in Italy they also use grappa as a medicine or as disinfectant to clean down the bar.

(v: Alcohol, Benders, Booty calls, Dipsomania)

GRASPING THE NETTLE

The truth is it hurts – most people would prefer to stay in bed for three days to watch the entire box set of *The Sopranos*, or stage the Trivial Pursuit Olympics to avoid doing it – but the anticipation is worse than the pain itself. The sting only lasts for a little while. So whether it's phoning your frenemy to apologize for last night's behavior or facing up to a bullying colleague at work – do it! It is difficult, but the more you are prepared to grasp the nettle, the easier it becomes.

(v: Money matters, Frenemies, Opening brown envelopes, Pensions)

GREEN EXERCISE

Just five minutes of exercise in a 'green space' can boost mental health. It could be walking, gardening, cycling, boating or horse-riding in locations such as a park, garden or nature trail. There is growing evidence that combining activities, such as roller skating or cycling, with nature boosts well-being. An even greater effect comes from exercising in a green-and-blue space – an area that also contains water, such as a lake or river. Our lives get out of balance living in an urban environment. As human animals we need to be in nature: feeling the ground beneath our feet, touching the grass. You need to see a horizon in a city of tall buildings. And we all need more vitamin D. Green exercise breaks the tyranny of the gym. Best of all, it's environmentally sound and it's free. Beautifully, the Japanese call it 'green bathing'.

(v: Ballooning weight, Comfort zone, Flow, Good stuff that's free)

✑

GREEN LIVING

This is very popular. However, recyling your batteries may not be enough to save the planet. We need big sweeping international change, radical policies and unswerving politicians, who are prepared to make difficult and unpopular decisions, now, in order that our grandchildren can live in a viable world. Time to demonstrate.

(v: Demonstrations, Eat your greens, Get involved, Green exercise)

✑

GREER, GERMAINE [ICON]

'You're only young once, but you can be immature forever.'

✑

GRIEF

'Don't grieve. Anything you lose comes around in another form.'

– RUMI

'Grief is a process, not a state.'
– ANNE GRANT
(v: Age of grief, Bereavement)

GUESTS (HOW TO BE A GOOD ONE)

The Chinese say that, rather like fish, guests go off after three days. There is definitely something in this. A good guest cannot be dreary and spoil the fun. Good guests bring a bottle of wine/ flowers/chocolate/something homemade if invited over for dinner. You will have already been keeping a keen ear out for tips, so you know what your host or hostess will really like. Good guests offer to walk the dog, load the dishwasher, and go on any trip proposed, even if they don't want to. They do not discuss their personal health, or anyone who is dying. If people go pink when you share your views on the Taliban, drop it, and go back to talking about some foodie phenomenon, or the latest wind turbine.

Clean the bathroom after use and air your room. Fling compliments around about the house, including 'God how do you manage to do all this?' Leave by 4:30 p.m. on a Sunday and always send a thank-you letter and all should be fine.

One 'killer-guest-stroke' was witnessed at an impromptu picnic in Devon. It involved a cool box, containing vodka, tomato juice, sherry, horseradish, Worcestershire sauce, Tabasco and celery salt, being unexpectedly produced from the boot of the car. Complete with two bags of ice. The devil, as they say, is in the detail.

❧

GUILLEM, SYLVIE [ICON]

'Having limits to push against is how you find out what you can do'.

❧

GUILT

Guilt is a woman-shaped word and can have the same poisonous, intense quality as envy or shame. We can feel guilty about almost anything – for being ambitious, for neglecting our family, skipping the gym, for lying about buying that new dress. But as many psychotherapists will tell you, guilt is not a real emotion. It's the default position we occupy when we won't accept the truth about our real feelings. Obviously we do things that upset people, such as breaking your sister's vase. You know you didn't do it on purpose, so logically you should have no reason to feel guilty about it. Yet you can't stop beating yourself up about your clumsiness, and how you could have avoided it. Now the question becomes: what does feeling guilty do for you? Is it secretly oddly comforting?

(v: Truth)

❧

GYNOCRATS

These are men who dig strong women and would rather hang out in all-female company. They have no problem with women taking the lead or having the best lines. These are the men you want at your top table.

Gynocrat comes from the noun gynocracy or gynaecocracy: a government or society ruled by women. Though more often found in myth and science fiction, matriarchal societies have existed through time, including the all-female Amazon culture reported by Herodotus (484-425 BC). For many years 'gynocracy' was a pejorative word used by antifeminist men to describe 'angry wimmin' who wanted to take over the world, after doing the washing and ironing, presumably.

But all that changed in 2009 when novelist, author of *The Rachel Papers*, and father of three daughters, Martin Amis, outed himself as a gynocrat. In fact, Martin added helpfully: 'I was quoted by, I'm pleased to say, Germaine Greer, as saying that all men should be locked up until they're 28. Boot camp. That would knock some sense into them. We're terrible. We can't help it!'

It's a heartening reappraisal by a former *enfant terrible*.

(v: Middle-aged novelists, Top table)

HADID, ZAHA [ICON]

'You really have to have a goal. The goal posts might shift,
but you should have a goal. Know what it is you want to find out.'

HAIR

'Sometimes I think not worrying about your hair anymore
is the secret upside of death.'
– NORA EPHRON

(v: Blow-dries, Necessary vanity)

HAIR DYE

The ability to dye your hair has sort of changed everything. Before the fifties very few women dyed their hair and even in the seventies the artist Francis Bacon famously chose to touch up his roots with boot polish, but dye has been a massively liberating product for women, who almost as a matter of course all dye their hair at a certain age. Don't ever underestimate its restorative powers.

(v: You're only young twice)

∽

HAIRINESS

Wouldn't it be nice if we could all be a bit more grown-up about being hairy? Body hair is there for a reason. It protects the skin from chafing, transfers heat into and out of the body and absorbs drips and fluids. Plus denser areas of hair are sites of scent-releasing glands that trigger sexual attraction in others.

(v: Bikini wax, Brazilian, Necessary vanity)

∽

HAIR LOSS

Whether it's the result of stress, the menopause or chemotherapy, hair loss can feel depressing and undermining. Hair loss doesn't just affect the scalp, it can affect eyebrows, eyelashes, nasal hair and pubic hair. The lack of eyelashes and nasal hair are particularly irritating as it can mean you catch eye infections more easily and have a permanently runny nose.

The truth of the matter is it ain't fun and it's vital that you try and keep your spirits up, so perhaps now is the time to invest in that Hermès scarf you have always wanted (or a good fake). Or dig out your mum's retro-seventies Elizabeth Taylor–

style turban and add a sparkling paste brooch for extra panache. However, if you are not in the mood to make your hair loss a fashion feature, you can simply buy yourself a very good wig. Bravest of all is to shave your own head. Surely it's time for the return of the Rude Girl . . .

(v: Cancer buddy, Climacteric, Ward wear)

ભ

HANDBAGS

'I have this Ferragamo hot-pink bag that I adore. . . . I mean, how can you be unhappy if you pick up a big pink bag?'

– HILLARY CLINTON

God. Don't we love handbags? They are like sweeties for big girls or penises for women. All you need for a tip-top handbag collection is a good eye and a slightly impulsive nature. We have bought bags from all around the world: the best of the swag is a rather brilliant Louis Vuitton for ten dollars from a yard sale in Florida. Of course, you need all sorts of different handbags for different occasions. They don't all have to be super luxury items. All they need to do is catch your eye, cheer you up and be capable of carrying at least keys, cigs and a lipstick. Have a checklist when you move the contents of one to another.

(v: Elegance)

⚬⚬⚬

Handstand revolution

Doing a handstand against a wall can help you reset and recharge your metabolism for the day. It reverses gravity allowing much-needed rest for your legs and feet, it improves upper body and core strength and the rush of blood to the head is great for your face and skin. Forget dreary old weights and rowing machines, handstands remind us of when we were very young and filled with dreams.

(v: You're only young twice)

⚬⚬⚬

Handwritten letters

Letters were once the only way to conduct long-distance relationships. We waited weeks for them to arrive from pen pals or boyfriends who had gone to India in their gap year, kept them scented and beribboned in our knicker drawers (surely what they were invented for) and in return poured our hearts out onto paper-thin airmail letters or Basildon Bond writing paper – and practiced our best italic handwriting with beautiful fountain pens.

Sadly, in this new age of mass communication letters have lost some of their importance but, much as we all adore instant messaging, is anyone seriously backing up e-mails and tweets for posterity, apart from those rather frightening corporations in Silicon Valley? Are we convinced that the expression of our hearts and souls will not all be reduced to memory sticks? We still fantasize about long discursive letters. They're part of our emotional history. So go and find that dusty bottle of ink and get weaving.

Letters excel in conveying a true message. Whether it's a thank you, a love note, or for saying you are sorry in a way that is hard to ignore: for putting across the tricky, difficult, private or loving. Still feeling cynical? Go to the penultimate scene in *Persuasion* and you will change your mind.

(v: Affairs, Accepting invitations)

சொ

HANDYMAN

You need a handyman in your little black book because, try as you might, the battle with the drill and the spirit level may be *un peu de trop*. Give him a list and start with the most important task, especially if it involves the roof, then work your way down to the more cosmetic adjustments. Don't let him spend days doing paint effects when he can be putting up shelves. Because he can handle a hammer, you will naturally think he walks on water, so beware of having a 'cavewoman' moment. Make sure he clears up the debris before he moves on and, whatever you do, don't sleep with him or he will, ultimately, cease to be useful.

(v: Caveman moment)

Have you got the kit?

Although donning a pair of stockings and garters in a dusty tent in Coachella may not be your idea of fun it's not unsensible to be a little bit prepared for the booty call, the wild weekend away or just simply the romantic advances of the man you love. A lovely bit of kit or even just a beautiful bra, tucked away in the back of a chest of drawers quietly awaiting the right moment, can instill secret confidence.

(v: Affairs, Booty calls, Cinq à sept, Creative corsetry, Twice is polite)

(The) Heart

'It is only with the heart that one can see rightly.
What is essential is invisible to the eye.'
– Antoine de Saint-Exupéry

Heckling

Has its place. Make your target lazy politicians, they are three a penny.

(v: Demonstrations)

Hell

'If you are going through hell, keep going.'
– Winston Chruchill

HEMLINES

Supposedly the great economic indicator. When stocks are soaring, skirts rise to mini length. When markets head down, hemlines drop. But every woman is the arbiter of her own hemlines. Don't be bullied into wearing anything that makes you uncomfortable. Many of us prefer above-the-knee in winter and longer in summer when everyone starts baring flesh. As a rule of thumb you can probably go shorter than you think or chance a flirty dress, worn with a long jacket. But before interviews and dates, check out that optimum length by sitting in front of the mirror. There's nothing worse than the wrong sort of 'skirt drift'.

(v: Elegance, Frocks)

HEN NIGHTS

Time to make a stand against bunny ears and penis-shaped lollipops. Do you really want to spend a small fortune in a nightclub with people with whom you have nothing in common, bar the fact that you share a friend who happens to be about to get married? Ask any woman and she will have at least one story of hen-night-related humiliation. However, it is important to mark a rite of passage. There are far more grown-up ways to celebrate – especially if it's a case of late love. One friend organized a screening of her favorite film at the British Film Institute, followed by cocktails and supper at

Claridges. Another designed a brooch, worn by all the hens on their weekend away, to keep as a memento. Part of the pleasure of the modern hen night is making an age-old tradition fun, personal and a bit grown-up.

(v: Catching the bouquet)

HIGH HEELS

If you're normally a Converse All-Stars kind of girl, don't just roam off in a virgin pair of high heels and hope for the best. Hobbling is not the look you are aiming for. A little baby lotion around the edges of the shoes and a practice trot around the house are vital. You are aiming for an upright posture and a gracious gait. Jerry Hall suggests 'Think book on the head, and a light bounce in the walk'. Practice standing on tippy-toes to strengthen tootsies and this may be the moment to think expensive. A well-made pair of high heels will allow your body to rest slightly back on your heels, realign itself and balance accordingly, as opposed to a shoddily made pair of stilettos which will throw your hips and body weight forward. This will make you look like Jack Lemmon in drag in *Some Like It Hot*.

(v: Feet, Flats)

HOARDING VS. MESS

Hoarding can be quite a pejorative word, and if you are a hoarder you will find that you are often accused of being sentimental and untidy. Ignore men folk at this point. They love to throw things away because it's easier than tidying up. However, the total horror show of out and out clutter can be tackled with the aid of a steely eyed sibling or friend who will galvanize the clear up and help sort out the piles for 'clean', 'keep', 'store', 'charity shop' and 'chuck it out'.

Huge clear bags from places like IKEA cost a couple of dollars and mean you can stash away in the attic (or other grottos) clothes and shoes and other prized possessions that a darling daughter will adore to inherit when she comes of age. They ensure that all is clean and dry and will also be readily identifiable.

Buy plastic folders with about 40 pages, and file your newspaper cuttings, old photographs, tickets stubs and pressed flowers here. There is nothing nicer than keeping old diaries, love letters, writing poems, school reports and 'stuff '. So long as everything is clean and organized and parked in a suitable place, your children, grandchildren and/or godchildren will be the beneficiaries in due course.

(v: Good stuff that's free, Green living, Memory boxes, Passing stuff on)

ოჩ

HOLIDAYING WITH GIRLFRIENDS
(PLEASURES AND PITFALLS)

What could be nicer than a holiday with your best girl pal? No irritating relatives. No moody men. Just cocktails and fun. However, the bad news is, relations with friends can sometimes be strained to near breaking point by character traits you only begin to notice once you're on the road.

Do you have the same attitude to money? Do you both drink? What if one of you likes to be in bed by 9 p.m.? Will there be a clash between the beach and the art gallery? Will it be a disappointment if you don't meet charismatic men? Does she actually eat food at all? Even the best of friends can hide these sort of details from each other.

It's often better to do a mini-break or weekend away first, as a trial run. Many singletons are simply not used to spending 24 hours a day with another person, so tolerance can be sorely stretched. Your lovable taxi habit may be the very thing that brings her out in a cold sweat. Ditto her snobbery about contemporary art. Even the nicest people can end up arguing about table manners or when to open the car window.

Do discuss the following:

1. How much time will you spend together each day?
2. How far are you prepared to travel to your destination?
3. Do you want to share a room (factor in heat, snoring, possibility of seduction)?
4. Do you want an all-inclusive holiday offering hassle-free relaxation, or a self-catering apartment or villa?
5. Is sunshine important?
6. Do you want to drive while away?
7. Would you prefer to visit many places during the trip or stay in a single destination? Some of us get palpitations about packing up every two days!

(v: Anger)

උත්

HONEY

'If you want to gather honey, don't kick over the beehive.'
– DALE CARNEGIE

The ancient Egyptians considered bees the symbol of sacred femininity. Honey was also used for healing wounds and as a preservative (due to its antibacterial properties). Raw, unprocessed honey is a super-food that provides antioxidants, minerals, vitamins, amino acids . . . you name it. Stick to darker honey. The pollen from flowers that produce dark honey contains the most micronutrients. It's never been more fashionable to be an urban beekeeper: sign up for an apiarist course in your area. Those without gardens are using rooftops or balconies for their hives; or you can buy a fabulous plastic bee house structure. We particularly like those sexy hats with veils.

(v: Container gardens, Skin, Super-foods)

උත්

HONORARY GIRLS

Contrary to the film *When Harry Met Sally*, it is possible for men and women to be friends without erotic tension. There's a huge relief to hanging out with a male pal who understands your jokes, reads the same books, can give you impeccable advice on a shopping trip and can understand the dark arts though not practice them. As it happens, you wouldn't necessarily want him to. He's not competing with your girlfriends, rather he's part of the pack. Alpha males can stop sniggering at the back right now: being an honorary girl says nothing significant about sexuality but it does mean a man who gets you. Truly great and lasting platonic friendships are worth fighting for. And the more exposure you have to the way the opposite gender thinks, the better, but do watch out for his slightly green-eyed new wife. She may find your mutual, easy intimacy a threat and if she does, be merciful.

(v: Good husband material, Gynocrats, Top table)

⤮

HOPE

'Hope begins in the dark.'
– ANNE LAMOTT

Hope is possibly the most beautiful word in the English language. Hope is what keeps us going. Hope is the future and increasingly we are told to visualize our hopes so that they become a reality. In our darkest hours, hope gives us the possibility of a way forward. You need hope as much as you need the air that you breathe.

(v: Cancer buddy, Quests, Visualization)

HORMONES

Who hasn't gone to bed a perfectly sane woman and woken up as a wailing banshee? A hormone imbalance can have a drastic effect – causing everything from teenage acne to PMS, endometriosis, infertility, thyroid malfunction and depression. You are not being neurotic, this is a real thing. Don't let the doctor belittle you or treat you like a naughty schoolgirl.

From our teens to our late thirties, the battle is to keep our hormones on an even keel. According to women's doctor Marion Gluck: 'They work like a symphony together. When they are out of whack, we are out of whack.' An imbalance can cause bloating, irritability, low moods. By our late forties/early fifties, it's all in freefall. As women approach menopause, estrogen levels decline. We may opt for HRT or tailor-made bio-identical hormone replacement therapy, or simply sail through. But we need to be well informed about the options out there.

Hormones get unfair press – they really are a girl's best friend. They regulate every function in our bodies: from intellect to metabolism, from building bone strength to helping us cope with stress. They make us tick. They are the chemical messengers that continuously circulate in our bloodstream. They rule – and sometimes ruin – our lives. Rather thrillingly, no two women have the same endocrine system – like our fingerprint, it's totally unique.

(v: Eat your greens, Climacteric, Exercise, Vitamins)

ⱷ

HOSPITAL ETIQUETTE

Observe visiting times unless otherwise advised. Bring magazines, fresh fruit and sparkling water. Flowers are not allowed. Be up and light and tune in. Stay for as long as the patient requests and no longer. If close family arrive, say a cheerful farewell and leave without a fuss. It's not about you.

(v: Chemotherapy, Childbirth, Ward wear)

ⱷ

HOSPITALITY

'A house may draw visitors, but it is the
possessor alone that can detain them.'
– CHARLES CALEB COLTON

Generally, hospitality has nothing to do with money. It can be a fresh pot of coffee after a long journey. It can be a muffin and buttered toast with tea. It is the warm arm around your shoulder and a warm feeling in your tummy. It could be an offering of a bowl of soup, a spaghetti dish made from what's in the fridge, washed down with a bottle of rough red. Or, to warm the cockles of the heart, a slinky sloe gin with a dash of fizz. Whatever your notion of hospitality, provide food when there is hunger, drink when there is thirst and a metaphorical stable for the night. Hospitality is biblical in its resonance and one of the loveliest of human instincts.

(v: Cocktails, Cooking)

∾

HOUSEHUSBANDS

It sounds brilliant doesn't it? And some very high-powered women can run their lives because their husbands stay at home (sometimes in conjunction with a nanny) and look after the household. However, it takes a very particular kind of man who is able to subdue his ego in this manner without suffering side effects, often the most immediate being the loss of libido. In this scenario, Jung would argue that the animus/anima that are present in every archetypical partner relationship have fallen out of balance. If you and your partner are thinking about organizing life in this way, look long and hard into your hearts and minds and work through a shipwreck scenario before making a final decision.

(v: Jung, Shipwreck scenario)

∾

HOUSEWORK

'I think housework is far more tiring and frightening than hunting is, no comparison, and yet after hunting we had eggs for tea and were made to rest for hours, but after housework people expect one to go on just as if nothing special had happened.'

– NANCY MITFORD

(v: Cleaning, Flow)

I can't afford to buy cheap

This is extremely sound advice. Essentially, if your monthly budget is tight and you have little money to spare for nonessentials, it is better to save it and then spend it on a truly beautiful jewel-colored cashmere cardigan, an elegant pair of well-made boots, a gorgeous frock that can be dressed up or down, or a string of pearls, rather than blow it all on a load of stuff you will only wear once or twice. Similarly, an extra hundred dollars spent on a washing machine may give it an extra five years of life, ditto on a proper mattress or a well-sprung sofa. You will discover that even when something begins to fray at the edges, it remains beautiful and stylish and you will go to heaven for being so 'green'.

(v: Elegance)

∾

I DON'T

Divorce is very high on the list of top traumas, but those who bounce back quickest are the people who are able to manage their expectations. There is enormous fear of change and the unknown. It is scary to have to reassess who we are and who we might become. However, one of the most exciting and liberating things that can happen to a woman is to find herself on the road to postdivorce recovery. A lot of women over 40, having gone through a divorce, are having the time of their lives.

As divorce lawyer Vanessa Lloyd Platt says, 'In my mind the way forward is "Marriage Lite". It involves respect and companionship, but absolutely without taking one another for granted. It's not about picking up socks and sharing money and paying dreary bills. It's the enlightened choice for the emancipated woman and may even become "marriage à la mode".'

(v: Affairs, Companionship, Depression, Family therapy,
Grief, Lawyers, Money matters, Teenagers)

∾

IMAGINARY LOVE AFFAIRS WITH GAY BEST FRIENDS

It's incredibly easy to fall for your GBF without knowing it's happening (because he is so perfect), and fantasizing that it might just be reciprocated. Often it comes from a good place – as a way to avoid bruising masculinity or get over daddy damage. There's a reason we're all a bit in love with Tom Ford.

We dream of someone who gets our taste in films/books/ clothes. Who smells fabulous. And understands our strengths and weaknesses. But actually there's something self-destructive about desiring a man who doesn't want/need to sleep with women. And, of course, it's fatal if you're single. Poor, flawed straight men can never compete with GBFs for kindness and solicitude and treats and compliments. They set the bar way too high for heterosexuality. It's a lovely fantasy. But gay friends are just that. Friends.

(v: Gay best friends, Top table)

IMITATING FRENCH ACTRESSES

The French new wave cinema got it right. Brigitte Bardot, Catherine Deneuve and Jeanne Moreau were beautiful and powerful on screen and the latter two gave complex and intelligent performances in a range of films that might have been small in scale but were large in impact. But who has inherited their earth? A load of imitating, although admittedly very pretty, French actresses who use volatility, febrility, and an overwhelmingly self-conscious vulnerability to get their own way. Think back to Arletty, the star of one of the greatest films of all time, *Les Enfants du Paradis.* Fragile on the outside she had the inner steel of a paper-knife. When asked to comment on her alleged affair with a Gestapo officer she responded: 'My heart is French but my ass is international.' *Maintenant nous parlons!*

ပ⁓ဖ

IMPLANTS

'For this kind of money, they'd better be looking at them.'

– DOLLY PARTON ON PEOPLE WHO STARE AT HER SURGICALLY
ENHANCED BREASTS

Love them or hate them they remain an option. At some point you may need implants. A little bit of padding can help repair the wear and tear of the slightly beleaguered upholstery, which may have fed several babes and now could do with some perking up. With the best will in the world, once you've expanded from a 34C to 40D and back again, even the most hopeful exercise regime won't get you pinging back. If you want to have implants and have the means to do so and you think it will make you feel tip-top, then frankly you owe it to yourself. Do your research, go and see the best consultant available and see if you can talk to somebody who has experienced the same procedure.

Beware, implants are not a teeny undertaking but, for many, a couple weeks of severe discomfort may be worth it if you finally have the chest you are happy with. After all, it will last you a lifetime.

(v: Boobs, Bras, Cosmetic surgery, Creative corsetry)

ပ⁓ဖ

IN BLUEBEARD'S CASTLE

One of the most devastating leitmotifs in Bartók's opera *Duke Bluebeard's Castle* is the sound of the sighing of the dead wives who have been incarcerated within the castle walls. Widowers can be a very attractive proposition to Dangerous Women: they are vulnerable, often deeply traumatized and desperate to love again as quickly as possible and they often come with ready-made families and nice houses. But beware, dead wives, however imperfect, can cast a long shadow. There will be enormous expectations all around, which are hard to meet, and the man who will eventually emerge from behind the widower you fell in love with may be a very different and much more diffcult proposition.

(v: Good husband material, Stepchildren)

⚜

INCEST AND FOLK DANCING
'Try anything once apart from incest and folk-dancing.'
– SIR THOMAS BEECHAM

⚜

INDEPENDENT BOOKSHOPS

In a world of three-for-two, it's extremely tempting just to shop at the retail blockbusters. But indie booksellers have a breadth of knowledge that's hard to match. They'll recommend new authors, order a long-forgotten title, even give you a mini-bibliotherapy session if you're bored by your bookshelf.

If you value authors – and the small independent presses who discover them – it's a nice gesture to pay full price. Independent book and record shops matter.

They offer expertise and choice. So shut down the laptop and walk across the road to a proper shop.

(v: Be well informed)

ᭈ

INFINITE VARIETY

'Variety's the very spice of life, That gives it all its flavor.'
– 'THE TASK', WILLIAM COWPER

'Age cannot wither her, nor custom stale Her infinite variety.'
– *ANTONY AND CLEOPATRA*, II. I., WILLIAM SHAKESPEARE

(v: Adventure, Comfort zone, Get out of a rut and get involved)

ᭈ

INSOMNIA

For long-term sufferers, there is nothing more infuriating than the person you meet at a party who tells you that as soon as their head hits the pillow they sleep for an uninterrupted eight hours and then in the same breath goes on to recommend an alternative practitioner who will sell you an expensive but useless cure.

Rather like Persephone and/or Count Dracula, insomniacs live part of their life in a silent, dark, disorienting and often isolating world. The condition is, of course, self-fulfilling: the more you don't sleep the more you don't sleep. Reams and reams have been written about insomnia, its causes and possible solutions. However, there is no doubt that worry, stress, grief, depression, a disastrous love life or troublesome teenagers can all contribute to this condition, so addressing and dealing with these factors, rather than simply 'coping' with them, can be enormously helpful. Top tips for 'through thick and thin' insomniacs are as follows:

1. Establish a strict bedtime routine.

2. Only use your bed for sex and sleeping.

3. Cut out alcohol (although a counterintuitive suggestion is to drink a glass of chilled white port at three in the morning).

4. See the glossary for suggested reading.

5. If you are really desperate, go and see your doctor: there are some finely tuned meds available that will nudge you toward 'the land of nod'.

Two final reassuring thoughts. Prior to the Industrial Revolution it was commonplace in the summer for people to rise at three or four o'clock in the morning and eat, work or play and then go back for a snooze before getting up to face the day. Some mystics believe that three a.m. is the holiest time of the day. It's known as the 'The Waking Hour.'

(v: Catnapping, Depression, Grief, Meds, Persephone, Sunglasses)

INSTINCT

Sometimes we just know someone is not to be trusted, or that a particular flat or house will make us happy for the next twenty years.

Feminine instincts are women's natural way of knowing. In a male-dominated work world, they are often perceived as inferior or too subjective. But we should listen to that gut feeling that something is totally right – or wrong. Thinking too much can actually lead you to make the wrong decision. Like a computer, the rational brain has limitations. It can handle a certain amount of information at any given moment, but if you give it more than that you can overwhelm it.

It turns out that in what scientists call 'our internal supercomputer', emotions that emerge from our unconscious minds tend to reflect more information than our rational minds.

The best times to trust your emotional, intuitive thought process are in situations in which you've had a lot of experience, such as buying a car or getting married.

Listening to your heart doesn't involve doing more, but doing less – so set your mind free.

&

INSURANCE

You can insure anything. If you are finalizing a divorce, it is interesting to know that you can insure your soon-to-be-ex-husband's maintenance payments in the event of his death. Think about it.

(v: Cars, I don't, Money matters, Things that make your life easier)

✍

Intensify the pleasure

Deferring gratification is seen as a marker of positive adult behavior, but it also intensifies the pleasure. So whether you're deferring sex or a cup of tea it gives you time to think about the choice you make and whether it's the right one.

(v: Deferment of pleasure, Mercy fuck)

✍

Introducing people

'Do you know so and so?' Introducing friends to one another is a very generous thing to do, and everybody knows it. Introducing people at a party should be second nature, though it can be a teeny bit annoying if you are on the prowl and have just started chatting someone up to be interrupted midflow and forced to smile politely at somebody new. So if you are a long-term 'introducer' be sensitive to the social context. However, it's a pretty straightforward skill to acquire. 'Do you know such and such? Do you two know each other?' Conversation will easily follow and the world will somehow be a better place thanks to you.

(v: Hospitality, Reading groups)

✍

It's a gift

Although we live in modern times there is, particularly as you get older, quite a strongly disapproving clique who say one-night stands are bad for morale. This may be the case and nobody respects a man who simply takes advantage but, very occasionally, if an offer comes your way, think about taking it. If you have just come out of a long-term relationship it may help you to break the spell, if you just want some fun and a bit of companionship what is so bad about that? Consider ignoring the moral majority, ensure you use effective contraception and don't harbor long-term expectations. After all is said and done, it's a gift.

(v: Committed bachelors, Orgasms, Think like a man, Twice is polite)

✿

It's a girl

'One day . . . the girl and the woman shall exist with her name
no longer contrasted to the masculine; it shall have a meaning in
itself. It shall not bring to mind complement or limitation –
only life and being: the feminine human being.'
– *Letters to a Young Poet*, Rainer Maria Rilke

Girls may be the new boys. Gender disappointment is not formally recognized in its own right and is mostly treated as a feature of post-natal depression. Most of those affected long for daughters and seize eagerly on natural methods to sway gender. These include sleeping with a lime-soaked tampon (to increase vaginal acidity); eating plenty of dairy products (a high calcium intake is anecdotally linked to having girls) and carefully timing intercourse for just before or just after ovulation (i.e. outside peak fertility, to favor slower, more resilient female sperm over live-fast, die-young male sperm). The fun aspect of this is to have lots of good sex in the week running up to ovulation and a few days postovulation. The great step forward is that the western world is a fabulous place to be born a girl. Let's make it so for the other half of the world's population.

(v: Babies, Fertility, Godmothers)

ew

. IT SEEMED LIKE A GOOD IDEA AT THE TIME
Well, if it seemed like a good idea at the time, it probably was. We all need to kick off our killer heels from time to time and letting off steam can be good for the mind, body and spirit, but if it results in sleeping with your best friend's boyfriend, betting your holiday money on a horse in the Grand National at odds of 250 to 1, or setting fire to your boss's desk in a moment of frustration, you may have some letters of apology to write and some further thinking to do.

(v: Benders, Drunk-dialing, Regrets)

ew

IT'S NOT ALL ABOUT YOU
We can all get paranoid about other people's motives. But so often, it's not actually about us. The boss is in a bad mood because his/her baby didn't sleep last night. Your friend 'ignored' you at the party because an awkward situation arose with her

husband. Instead of rushing to get upset about a perceived slight, try and look coolly at the situation. Or even ignore it altogether until you get a proper explanation. It can be a relief not to be the focus of everyone's attention. Most people are too busy worrying about their own personal problems to notice yours. In our desire to be sensitive and 'fit in', we can make ourselves rather more important than we actually are. Time to stop playing the drama queen.

(v: Self-pity)

ᨀ

IT'S OKAY TO WATCH TV

Don't knock it. TV is a great resource. It's educational, informative and entertaining and a shared love of a particular program is a way of connecting with your tribe. It's great if you just need to chill out and relax; brilliant if you are getting over a love affair . . . there's nothing like a costume drama or three to take your mind off it, and good for infinite vistas if your budget and your mindset won't let you leave your armchair. However, don't veg out on a 24/7 basis. That's the definition of depression.

(v: Be well informed, Grief, Good stuff that's free)

J

JEALOUSY

A really insidious and destructive emotion. Nothing good can come of it. If it rears its ugly snake-shaped head deconstruct it immediately, with some degree of compassion, as to why you feel jealous in the first place.

(v: Frenemies, Schadenfreude)

JEWELRY

Whether it's a vintage silk floral corsage or a fabulous bit of bling, brooches are a form of personal symbolism. Each tells a story of its own – and they're great ice breakers at parties. You can use one to dress up an inexpensive outfit. Or hide behind one on a down day. Whether it's a fabulous bracelet, or Coco Chanel's double rope of pearls, jewelry is the best form of armor. Who cares if you're wearing the black tent dress again?

(v: Ballooning weight, Pearls)

༒

JOY

*'We should all do what, in the long run, gives us joy, even if it is
only picking grapes or sorting the laundry.'*
– E. B. WHITE

༒

JUNG

*'Even a happy life cannot be without a measure of darkness,
and the word happy would lose its meaning if it were not balanced
by sadness. It is far better to take things as they come along with
patience and equanimity.'*
– CARL GUSTAV JUNG

If Freud is for the first half of your life, Jung is for the second.
His interpretations of archetypes, myths and symbols are rich,
informative and filled with non-judgemental insight into the
stories of our lives.

(v: Be well informed, Depression, Dreams, Freud)

Karma

What goes around comes around. Karma is the cosmic realignment of good and evil in the universe.

(v: Charitable giving, Hospitality)

Keep your diary full

Plan ahead and make sure you've got a week to look forward to. Call the friend who makes you howl with laughter. Invite out the most promising contact you've made in the last seven days – buy two tickets for a film or play, or invite them for a simple supper. Don't turn down a promising invitation – especially if you have just been dumped, rejected or fired. There are plenty more fish in the sea.

(v: Hospitality)

KEEPSAKES AND TALISMANS

Little treasures. Engraved with dates and messages. Mementos or stones or charms that are pertinent only to you. String them on thin chains to make dainty necklaces and exquisite bracelets. You can carry these with you for good luck and/or pass them on to people you love.

(v: Sentimentality, Tattoos)

KIND MIRRORS

Your ego is only as good as your last mirror. Find your favorite one and stick with it.

(v: Necessary vanity)

KINDNESS

'Kindness is the greatest form of wisdom.'
– THE TALMUD

It expands the soul. And it's the best anti-aging beauty tip we can give!

(v: Good stuff that's free, Karma)

KNEES

Cycling, walking, going on the Power Plate, cross-training or swimming.

You've got to do everything you can to look after these babies as they are the lynchpins of your skeleton. The key is to keep the supporting muscles strong, to keep the kneecap in place, and able to remain supple and agile. Slinky knees can be yours. When in doubt, take up tap dancing.

(v: Bones, Cycling, Outdoor exercise, Riding, Tap dancing)

LASER SURGERY
Really helpful for bad eyesight, scarred skin and painful veins.
(v: Skin, Veins)

LATE LOVE
(v: Accepting invitations, Little black book, Open mind, Salad days)

LATENESS
'Punctuality is the courtesy of kings.'
– LOUIS XVIII

There's nothing grown-up about being late. It wastes other people's time and goodwill. To the very punctual your lateness is a mark of arrogance. To your therapist, lateness is a sign that you are surreptitiously stealing time from other people thus testing their loyalty. But punctuality freaks need to be flexible too – no one should be bullied into a deadline they can't meet. If you are the punctual type, use the extra time to catch up on other things or maybe just dream a little.

(v: Kindness)

LAUGHTER

'The appreciative laughter of a girl, however charming, is not to be compared to the deep pleasurable laughter in which a woman of intelligence can envelop a man.'
– *DAILY MAIL*, 25 JANUARY 2010, HOWARD JACOBSON

The good news is that 100–200 belly laughs a day will burn off 500 calories and tone your stomach. Laughter is a natural painkiller and inspires the immune system to create white T-cells, commonly called 'happy cells'. It's especially good for controlling Type A personalities!

(v: Female comedians)

LAWYERS
Don't ring your divorce lawyer until you've stopped crying.

(v: Divorce, Money matters)

‿‿

LAZY MATH GIRL

*'Computers are like Old Testament gods; lots of
rules and no mercy.'*

– JOSEPH CAMPBELL

Apparently the average punter only uses, at best, about two percent of her computer's capacity, but that is predicated on the fact that you understand computer technology at all. Essentially, if you dream of becoming a Web-maiden you need to understand and acquire a system of logic, which is frankly easier said than done if you were a lazy math girl at school – and most of us were. Essentially, we were all too busy fantasizing about Lord Byron to bother with basic algebra (unlike his daughter Ada Lovelace, coinventor of the computer). In recent times it has been pointed out that this is not necessarily our fault. Had the mathematical conundrums been invested with psychological importance, e.g. 'If your sister's female cousin has five siblings, three of them girls, how many daughters does your aunt have?', as opposed to, 'There are three men laying a railway track . . .', we might have got somewhere. As it is we have to rely on the kindness of work colleagues, teenagers and godchildren to get us through.

(v: Relativity, Technology)

ᏪᏅ

LE GADGET

Princess Di's code name for her vibrator was le gadget. According to her biographers she often had it delivered incognito in front of foreign ambassadors.

Once upon a time 'marital' aids were embarrassing and unaesthetic. But the days of 12-inch phallic-shaped vibrators brought out with sniggers at hen nights are defiantly over. From cones, pebbles and balls, to rabbits and scorpions, you don't have to hide them away in your drawer. Some are solo toys, others are to share with a partner. Cool furniture designers Tom Dixon and Marc Newson have designed beautifully shaped, vibrating sculptures. Having a vibrator doesn't mean you're sad and lonely. They're just as likely to be given as gifts between girlfriends, couples and even as wedding presents – the new scented candle, if you like. The good thing about the 'new openness' is vibrators no longer threaten men, who have come to see them as helpful. It's also fine if you have no interest in acquiring one whatsoever.

ᏪᏅ

LEARNING TO LOVE YOURSELF
'Nobody can make you feel inferior without your consent.'
– ELEANOR ROOSEVELT

(v: Accepting compliments, Confidence)

◦◦◦

LEAVING THE PARTY

I used to think,
Loving life so greatly,
That to die would be
Like leaving the party
Before the end.
Now I know that the party
Is really happening
Somewhere else.

– 'LEAVING THE PARTY', ANONYMOUS

Leaving the party is hard to do. The only grain of comfort is that a billion people have done it before you, so you can too.

(v: Cancer buddy, Hair loss, Making a will, Memory boxes, Ward wear)

◦◦◦

LEGS (GET THEM OUT)

Yours are beautiful. No matter how short, wide or gangly. Whether they're standing, walking, jumping, running or kicking ass, legs are freedom. So love your legs, they're your best friends and the surest escape hatch. Any room, any situation that's not up to muster, just walk out. Elegantly, defiantly, surely. Stand up, give your legs a little shake and glide away.

(v: Emergency exit, Exercise, Legs)

❧

LESBIAN BED DEATH

When it comes to forming a healthy, sustaining, emotionally intelligent relationship it might seem like the answer to one's prayers finally to fall in love with another woman. However, one tiny word of warning, once the excitement of discovering a different aspect to one's sexuality has worn off you may discover that you are not a lesbian after all.

(v: Baby dykes)

❧

LET IT GO

'There it be so here goes.'
– UNDER THE GREENWOOD TREE, THOMAS HARDY

'The heart gives, the fingers just let it go.'
– NIGERIAN PROVERB

❧

LIBRARIES

Are worth fighting for. They offer timeless knowledge, nurture our chance to reflect on life and are free to use, providing books for everyone. They are also a neutral space, a refuge in a busy world and, in the roaringly acquisitive 'global market' in which we live, they are a symbol of civic pride and representation of the antiquated, but vitally important, belief in learning and education for learning and education's sake.

(v: Be well informed, Good stuff that's free)

∿

LIPSTICK
'The red badge of courage.'
– MAN RAY

At the turn of the century cosmetics were often sold 'under the counter'. Selfridges was the first department store to openly sell powder and rouge, thus transforming the social acceptability of makeup. During the 1910s, many women in the suffragette movement wore bright red lipstick as a symbol of their defiance. Suffragette leaders like Elizabeth Cady Stanton and Charlotte Perkins Gilman argued that wearing lip rouge was an emblem of women's emancipation. Nowadays lipstick is the ultimate credit-crunch indicator. Economists believe that during hard times people forgo extravagant purchases, such as cars and holidays, and spend their money on small luxuries. During the Second World War it was considered women's patriotic duty to wear lipstick. Nowadays you may not have to chain yourself to the railings to get your point across but please wear your Mac Russian Red with pride.

(v: Art of makeup, Mascara)

∿

LITTLE BIT OF WHAT YOU FANCY DOES YOU GOOD
Whether it's the occasional cigarette, a Crunchie or sloping off to the cinema in the afternoon, honor these small and entirely harmless whims and fancies. Nobody else is going to do it for you.

(v: Variety is the spice of life)

ৎ⌒

LITTLE BLACK BOOK

We've all got one of these, but we need to dust it down and freshen it up a little from time to time. If necessary, swap entries with a friend. Remember, however, to pay the price of a bottle of champagne or a finder's fee of $40 for a fella, especially one who turns out to be good husband material. Come on ladies, share and share alike.

(v: Good husband material)

ৎ⌒

LITTLE WHITE LIE

Sometimes truth is a luxury that you can't afford. If you are intending to lie only tell 97% of the truth.

(v: I can't afford to buy cheap, Kindness)

ৎ⌒

LIVING IN THE MOMENT
(v: Flow, Instinct)

ৎ⌒

LODGERS

Very useful they are in times of financial trouble. However, you do need to set some ground rules. You are not there to be a cleaner or to run a cheap hotel. Give them their own cupboards in the kitchen and bathroom. Provide bed linen if you wish, but shared use of the washing machine can be annoying. Three golden rules: ask them to clean up after themselves and request payment on time and in cash, and you'll be fine.

(v: I don't, Money matters)

உ௭ௐ

LONG-HAUL TRAVEL
Comfortable knickers are vital.
(v: Adventure, Camiknickers)

உ௭ௐ

LOSING THINGS
'The art of losing isn't hard to master; so many things seem filled with the intent to be lost.'
– ELIZABETH BISHOP

Losing things may be one of your special skills. If it is, you probably drive your nearest and dearest mad with your obsessive search for lost reading glasses, keys, theater tickets, pearls, scarves and designer sunglasses . . . The phrase, 'I know I put it somewhere safe', will have a hollow ring even to you, but losing things as a character trait may signify deeper concerns. In particular, if we have lost a parent or sibling at a very young age we may set up a repetitive losing-and-finding psychodrama that allows us to sustain the belief that one day we will find that person again. Whatever the underlying causes for your forgetfulness, with a little bit of effort, you can put some basic strategies in place that will make your life easier. Sadly, experience tells us that however strict you are about putting your ultra-cool sunglasses back in their case and back into your bag you will eventually lose them. This is the strange universal law of very expensive sunglasses.

(v: Pearls, Sunglasses)

⌘

Loss

"'But I think she would have been happy with Fabrice," I said. "He was the great love of her life you know." "Oh, dulling," said my mother sadly. "One always thinks that. Every, every time."'

– *THE PURSUIT OF LOVE*, NANCY MITFORD

(v: Age of bereavement, Grief, Insomnia)

⌘

Love

'Love conquers all; let us also yield to love.'

– VIRGIL

'At the touch of love, everyone becomes a poet.'

– PLATO

❧

'LOVE LETTERS'
'Where will all the love letters go
When cyberspace gobbles them up?
Can you stand tall beside that risky e-mail
When it is reduced to nothing at all.
Give me sly notes to add
To that knicker drawer cache
Give me secret love behavior, on some paper I can keep.
Leaving marks of blistering rendezvous,
The sight which makes me weep.'
– SARAH-JANE LOVETT

(v: Handwritten letters, Overuse of the Internet, Technology)

❧

LOVERS
'Alice: I don't love you anymore. Goodbye.
Dan: Since when?
Alice: Since now. Just now.'
– *CLOSER*, PATRICK MARBER

(v: Affairs, Arrangement, Cinq à sept)

MAD WOMEN

Men very often like to describe women as 'mad'. It has long been the ultimate stick to beat a woman with. It is dismissive, pejorative, cruel and manipulative. It is a way of making a woman doubt her own faculties and it is also a clever way of fueling rumor mills and helping a boyfriend or husband to pursue his own agenda. It is a prognosis that should not be trusted and can be very damaging, not just to the individual but also to children and extended family too. History, literature, opera and the psychiatric couch are littered with perfectly sane women who have had an adverse reaction to the male world and are being punished accordingly. The ultimate weapon of the patriarchy? 'She is mad because I say so'. Beware.

(v: I don't, Opera)

ᴄᴠᴛᴀ

MAGIC SPELLS

Whether you are seeking love, happiness or just some extra cash, they can sometimes work. The best days for magic spells are at full moon or at the summer or winter solstice. Essential ingredients are candles, scent, fresh herbs, salt and an elegant glass of something alcoholic. Be creative! You are the one who knows what you are trying to achieve. Lay everything out on a dinner plate and add extras such as love hearts, special ornaments, treasured letters – or, if you are feeling financially squeezed, a large check made out to yourself! If you are making a spell to help somebody else, take a photograph of it with your mobile and send it to the person in question. Two rules: let the candles burn out before you go to bed and don't take it too seriously.

(v: Candles)

ᴄᴠᴛᴀ

MAGICAL THINKING

Magical thinking is human thinking sometimes, it's successful thinking and it's an elegant way to marshal obsessions and compulsions around a good cause. Most of us go through life fueled by dreams, hopes and wishes – something that the cleverest computer will never be able to do for us. If we hitch our tics to a dream, or simply a magical paradigm. We beat that bus to the corner; we don't step on the cracks; we salute every number 7; we focus our minds on a positive outcome.

And the more frequently we call an outcome to mind, the more circumstance rallies behind it. It really does. Touch wood.

(v: Grief)

ოთ

MAKE THE MOST OF IT (*CARPE DIEM*)
'But at my back I always hear
Time's winged chariot hurrying near'
– 'TO HIS COY MISTRESS', ANDREW MARVELL

ოთ

MAKING A WILL

It is hard for people to make a will, particularly if you have a life-threatening illness, because it means facing up to your own mortality, but it's essential that you do, otherwise the government will just swipe the lion's share. If you have extensive assets it's probably best to get some good legal advice as to how to best share the loot. However, if you are on a tight budget just get a form and fill it in. You will need two friends or acquaintances to witness it. If you have particular wishes about the way you want your funeral to be conducted, it is a good idea to write a letter of intent, which can be kept alongside your will. However don't make your funeral arrangements too elaborate. It's really good for those you have left behind to think through what best reflects you and organize accordingly. It helps take their mind off sad things. Most important of all, if you have children under the age of 18 think carefully about who you would wish to be their legal guardians.

(v: Grasping the nettle, Insurance, Leaving the party, Money matters)

✍

MAKING IMPOSSIBLE DEMANDS ON YOURSELF

The omnipresence of digital technology has made slaves of us all. Pity the poor dame who, if she is not zipping around assuring one and all of her efficency in the meeting place, is on call to pick up everybody else's kids from school and have an emergency conference call with the board of governors while fund-raising for environmentally challenged frogs in Micronesia via the Internet or Googling to check rates for a yogatastic mini-break-cum-hen-night for the bride-to-be and 25 of her closest friends. A tool that was meant to bring freedom to all now seems to leave even less time for covering yourself in biscuit mix and getting your boots muddy. Unplugging your technology or leaving the grid altogether (which has been tried by the enviably hardy few with varying degrees of success) as yet remains unpunishable by law.

(v: Catnapping)

✍

MAMMOGRAM

These are X-rays of the breast to screen for breast cancer in women who have no signs or symptoms. Two images are generally taken of each breast to check there are no tumors. Mammograms often take place at a portable breast-screening unit (which frequently have no loos!) and are offered to women in their forties and above. To be repeated every one or two years, minimum. Don't delay.

A diagnostic mammogram is used to do a second check after a lump or sign or symptom has been diagnosed. This testing usually takes longer.

(v: Cancer buddy, Hair loss)

MANIFESTING A MAN

*'I wrote a list which was very precise, included in that
list was his ability to be kind, generous, financially solvent, noble,
strong, quick to laugh and slow to anger. A man that respects
women and loves his mother. Someone who would accept me for
who I am and what I am.
I used a new moon, as symbolic of a new beginning.
I ran a bath and added rose, jasmine and rosemary. I put a big
piece of rose quartz in the tub and began to visualize my husband.
I also made a commitment to the universe that I would become
much more flexible; flexibility bends rigidity. I stayed in the bath
for about a half an hour, got out and went to sleep with rosemary
sprigs under my pillow. I met my husband the next day.'*

– JOHNNIE FIORI

(v: Good husband material, Magic spells, Top table)

✎

MANNERS
(v: Accepting a compliment)

✎

MANTEL, HILARY [ICON]
*'I think for a woman to say that "I'm not a feminist"
is [like] a lamb joining the slaughterers' guild. It's just
empty-headed and stupid.'*

✎

MANTRAS (THINGS TO HELP YOU LIVE A GOOD LIFE)
It is useful to have a few calming and insightful sayings onhand
to get you through irritating, stressful or tough moments.
Sometimes even a boring platitude will do.

✎

MAP READING
Map reading was designed for men but the goddess of serenity
has now designed and sent us the GPS. So no more fighting in
the car. No more sweaty palms as you summon up the courage
to admit that yet again you have directed the designated driver
to take the wrong exit from the motorway, resulting in an
extra hour and a half on a 200-mile round trip. We repeat: the
emancipation, the liberty, the joy. So 'at the next exit take the
first left.' We most certainly shall.

MARTINIS

'I like to have a martini,
Two at the very most.
After three I'm under the table,
After four I'm under my host.'

– DOROTHY PARKER

THE VESPER MARTINI

(v: Alcohol, Benders, Booty calls, Drunk-dialling, Mercy fuck)

MASCARA

You'd be silly not to.

(v: Allure)

MASSAGE (ANY FORM)

Whether you're tired, lovelorn or simply out of touch with your body, there's something incredibly soothing about neutral touch from another human being. We all want to feel the warmth of a hand on our shoulder after a long day; a gentle stroke on our head in moments of difficulty. Massage allows you to switch off that nagging inner voice, unwind and breathe deeply and slowly. You will emerge blinking into the daylight but as languorous as a cat.

(v: Intimacy)

〰

MATERIAL GIRL

We all know women who are only motivated by money. They're great fun, keen to party, and quite like taking you along with them – particularly if they don't feel that you are a sexual threat. In their company you get the best restaurant table, slip past the velvet rope into the VIP lounge, and that can feel great for a limited period of time. But the truth is they are simply not to be trusted. In the end it's all about them and their upward trajectory, cf. Becky Sharp in *Vanity Fair*. They've always got their eye over your shoulder for richer pickings. And, funnily enough, you'll more often than not find yourself bankrolling them, in your role as the substitute man. It's boring that they don't see the point of earning their own living or that ultimately they give women a bad name.

(v: Frenemies)

〰

MATING IN CAPTIVITY

Can you continue to have great sex in a long-term relationship? Does good intimacy always make for great orgasms? And why do couples who care for each other very much often end up in a sexual desert? For psychotherapist Esther Perel (author of *Mating in Captivity*), the paradox of modern love is that the very forces that bind us – trust, mutuality, friendship – can kill our sex lives stone dead. Erotic desire is complex, messy and very often non-PC. The trick – to paraphrase Jerry Hall – is to see the bedroom and kitchen as very different places. Forget endlessly talking everything through and shared bathrooms. We need more distance, novelty and spontaneity. Be selfish, lustful. Create tension.

(v: Affairs, Divorce parties, Have you got the kit?)

∽

MATURITY
'The moment someone comes across as real and unstaged and comfortable, it has so much more power.'
– WOLFGANG TILLMANS, ARTIST

∽

MEDITATION
Through simple relaxation techniques we can learn to step off the treadmill. It only takes ten minutes a day and it doesn't matter if you don't have spiritual faith. Meditation is a free tool for stress relief. You don't need to chant or lie down; you can meditate on the subway – it's a good way to beat commuter stress. And the beauty is that it is both inexpensive and portable and scientifically proven to be a powerful defense against stress and anxiety.

Remember, if you are busy allow for one hour's meditation a day. If you are rushed off your feet allow for two!

1. Sit on a comfortable chair, close your eyes and take five deep breaths.

2. Let your mind have free rein. Don't feel guilt if you find yourself thinking about food, shopping – or sex.

3. Scan through your body and notice which parts feel comfortable and which feel tense. Each time your mind wanders bring it back to your breathing pattern. Simply be aware of your feelings, that way you can provide a framework for them to arise and fall away.

4. Focus on being at ease with whatever is happening in your mind. Open your eyes after ten minutes (it's worth setting a timer) and you should feel like you've had a great catnap.

(v: Flow)

ᘓᕦ

MEDS

'The art of medicine consists of amusing the patient
while nature cures the disease.'
– VOLTAIRE

There are plenty of useful meds for different ailments . . . and if you have to pop a pill once in a while, it doesn't mean that you will turn into an addled Stepford wife. For many a gal, Valium – or just call them calm pills – are useful for a fear of flying. You have to take half a pill for Europe and a whole one for a longer haul. It makes the flight very short indeed. A sympathetic doctor will give you these to help with the anxiety.

There are also pills to lose weight. Psychologically, battling on with battling the bulge can become a tad trying. A month of something speedy to give your regime a quick blast will set you back on track and you'll see real results.

Some use beta blockers or a tiny nibble of a sedative when having to speak to the old ex-hubby. A gin and tonic and a chaise longue can also help with this fairly gruesome task.

(v: Diets, Drugs, (the) Ex, Pain)

MEETING THE IN-LAWS

Guess who's coming to dinner?
(v: Courtesy, Exquisite listening, Grace, In-laws)

MEMBERS' CLUB

Traditionally a male preserve. If you have some spare funds it's a very good idea to join one. In particular, a members' club is a great way to meet friends, to entertain and amuse Americans, to stay over in town occasionally, to sit by yourself and write that novel. Take your mom, your lover, or, if you need to impress a new business contact or work colleague ever so slightly, a members' club is also a great place for old-fashioned grown-up business meetings where you want to make a good impression.

(v: Infinite vistas, Mentors)

MEMORY BOXES

Shoe boxes are wizard for this. Fill one with all your treasures, love letters, old passports and the crappy tape your first boyfriend made for you and a whole host of other stuff that only has meaning to you. If the long-term prognosis isn't great, start making these for your children.

(v: Cancer buddy, Emergency exit, Hair loss,
Leaving the party, Making a will)

MENTORS

We all need an elder sister-cum-fairy godmother. Someone who can help us take creative risks, move up the work ladder or offer a cool head when we're raging about injustice at work. The key is to think of someone who has complimentary skills to yours. If you are feeling adventurous set up your own networking group. Whether it's exchanging career tips, address book secrets or after-school coaching for the kids, there are lots of ways to peer monitor.

(v: Members' club)

MERCY FUCK

Urban myth has it that this term was coined by an episode of *Sex and the City*, and now in everyday use. But wherever it came from, to request a 'mercy fuck' from somebody is not the action of a tragic woman, but of somebody who recognizes sexual attraction and thinks of themselves as an equal. Usually associated with funerals and breakups; ask and you will be rewarded. But do remember that at some point the favor may need to be reciprocated.

(v: Bachelors, Booty calls)

ぐらく

MESS
(v: Muddling through)

ぐらく

METABOLISM
(v: Cider vinegar, Diets, Eat your greens, Super-foods)

ぐらく

MICROFINANCE
'. . . these millions of small people with their millions of small pursuits can add up to create the biggest development wonder.'
– PROFESSOR MUHAMMAD YUNUS, MANAGING
DIRECTOR OF GRAMEEN BANK

Micro-finance is a way of making financial resources available to the poorest people and a brilliant way in which you can help a woman in the developing world set up a business and support her family. Check it out.

(v: Charitable giving, Karma)

ぐらく

MIDDLESCENTS
Once upon a time MAWs (middle-aged women) wore wooly hats and sensible wellingtons. But middlescents aren't letting go of the boyfriend jeans and sequins just yet. Middlescence is officially the years when you are in-between your promising twenties and the grey wastelands of middle age.

Middlescents know that they are no longer young, and that they can't party to 4 a.m. without a gargantuan hangover, but they still dress and behave as if their hipster years aren't over and they always act as if they are having fun. Poster girls for middlescence include Helena Bonham Carter – who seems never happier than when she is wandering around in a bonkers dress with tousled hair. She always looks like she's having a good time.

Middlescents do 'casual' and 'eccentric', but never scruffy. They know you have to choose your face or arse, but they have proper haircuts and a beautician on call to keep skin in good nick. They also like the occasional pedicure and may have experimented with false eyelashes. As far as families and careers go, it's anything to convert boredom into fresh energy.

(v: Comfort zone, Portfolio careers)

Midlife crisis

Generally associated with the male of the species – but women are increasingly subject to midlife crises too. Whether it's because your children are leaving home, your once vibrant partner won't leave the house without an umbrella or you have just bought yourself a Harley-Davidson, you may find yourself challenged in the middle of life's journey. Depression, lack of purpose, ballooning weight or developing a massive crush on the barista in the local Starbucks are common symptoms. It will pass but it's a day at a time.

MINOGUE, KYLIE [ICON]

'Having had cancer, one important thing to know is you're still the same person at the end. You're stripped down to near zero. But most people come out the other end feeling more like themselves than ever before.'

(v: Cancer buddy, Hair loss, Leaving the party, Memory boxes, Visualization)

MIRREN, HELEN [ICON]

'The trick in life is learning how to deal with it.'

It's a bit mean of Helen Mirren to get even more beautiful as she gets older, but it's also inspiring. Why not try it?

(v: Childfree, Jealousy, Waist)

MISSED OPPORTUNITIES

Gosh. It's hard to bump into the man at the Christmas pantomime with his lovely young wife and three tiny tots and realize that he was the 'one'.

(v: The man I should have married)

ભ્ટ્ર

MISTRESSES
'Marrying your mistress creates a vacancy.'
– JAMES GOLDSMITH

You might know one, your husband might have one or you might be one.

(v: Affairs, An arrangement)

ભ્ટ્ર

MODERN FAMILIES
(v: I don't, In Bluebeard's castle, Teenagers, Stepchildren)

ભ્ટ્ર

MOJO
It's still there, we promise, even if your house looks like a pigsty.

(v: Midlife crisis)

ભ્ટ્ર

MOLES
Are gorgeous, provocative and divine, cf. *The Wicked Lady* or Cindy Crawford. But if for any reason they begin to enlarge, become raised or itchy, please go to your doctor and get them checked out.

ભ્ટ્ર

MOMMY BORES
You were not the first and you won't be the last, so ladies take a deep breath and put a sock in it. Motherhood is not supposed

to be a competition and you will not win an Olympic Mommy Medal if your children are only allowed to eat hummus and wear socks made of hemp. Your only achievement will be people yawning behind your back at parents' evening and giving you a wide berth at parties.

(v: Babies, Self-obsession)

ఊ

MONEY MATTERS

Women's much misunderstood relationship with money is explained by the fact that consumer spending throughout history was one of the few ways women could exert their power, influence and choice, even if they didn't have the vote. The financial services sector is only beginning to wake up to the fact that women in the modern world are earning a living and may, in some cases, have considerable spending power but little experience or knowledge about pensions, insurance, savings or investments. Amazingly, recent research shows that most women rely on their male partner for advice and unbelievably in some cases on their ex-partner. This is insane. There is no excuse. Seek independent financial advice at all times and if your financial advisor is a woman, so much the better.

*(v: Debt, Grasping the nettle, I don't, Insurance,
Opening brown envelopes)*

იდა

MOOD LIGHTING

One quick way to sex up your life.

(v: Candles, Kindness)

იდა

MORAL HIGH GROUND

Don't take it. Ever. It's deeply unattractive.

(v: Grace)

იდა

MORTALITY

'You only live once, but if you do it right, once is enough.'
– MAE WEST

'It's no use reminding yourself daily that you are mortal:
it will be brought home to you soon enough.'
– ALBERT CAMUS

იდა

MOTHERS

It is probably not until you actually experience or witness what
it is to be a mother that you begin to realize what they do and
go through. Whatever your mother is like, or was like if she is no
longer with you, the chances are that she tried to do her best for
her babies, as all mothers do. Her maternal instinct would have
compelled her to walk through fire, take the food from her own

mouth, sleep on cardboard and know no fear in order to feed and clothe her children. The concern that a mother has for her young is monumental. She only wants the best for you.

So now it's your turn – buy the chocolates, bring the flowers and pick up any clothes and books you think might suit her. Be thoughtful and call with news. She's probably even got a mobile phone and is into texting and e-mailing in a sort of Morse code. Good for her and lovely for the grandchildren. Invite her to stay, it's your turn to take her out now. Try and work out how many hours you can rub along for without going into meltdown on both sides. Remember all the squillion selfless things she's done for you, and try to make her happy.

(v: Daughters, Family therapy, Sisters, Sons)

ⴰ

MOTIVATION
'I am not a has-been. I am a will be.'
– LAUREN BACALL

'. . . never give up then, for that is just the place and time that the tide will turn.'
– HARRIET BEECHER STOWE

Know yourself and go for it.

ベみ

MUDDLING THROUGH

If you are feeling overwhelmed and your sense of self-worth is at an all-time low, try the 'five things mantra'. Simply write down five things you need to do each day, and do them. You'll find that life begins to take shape again. You may not find a cure for cancer, but if you take this rule to heart you will knock twenty-five things off your dreary-things-to-do list in a month. That's a result! Then you can give yourself a well-earned drink or treat yourself to a jasmine tea truffle.

(v: Chocolate, Feminism, Flow, Self-pity)

ベみ

MUSIC

With apologies to Shakespeare, but 'If music be the food of love, play on', and on and on and on. Everyone has a song that has changed their lives and most people have the soundtrack of their life cf. Desert Island Discs, which will evoke all sorts of perfect or not so perfect times. Share it around. No matter what the device, windup or digital, tinny speakers or surround-sound, turn it on, turn it up, and let the good times roll. Your life simply wouldn't be as much fun without it.

NAME-DROPPING
'David Bowie says "never name-drop."'
– KATE MORRIS

NARCISSUS

You will have come across one or two of these on your travels. It's worth recognizing the type when faced with him or her. Though, interestingly, it's usually a him. A Narcissus will tell you that he has been in love 'twenty times' but when push comes to shove, it turns out he has never been in a meaningful relationship. A Narcissus is often in a surface relationship with his good looks instead. The women in his life have no real form or shape and can only echo what he says back to him because he is unable to allow anybody a separate, unique identity. So while you may feel badly treated by a Narcissus, don't take it personally, he is far too busy looking at his own reflection in the mirror to worry about your feelings. He has no ill intention.

(v: Committed bachelors, Complete wankers)

ও

NAVY BLUE

"Any color as long as it's navy."
– JEAN MUIR

Wearing navy blue is a breeze. The most flexible color in the fashion spectrum, it can look pulled together yet slightly sassy, smart but at the same time very Bohemian. Think fisherman's smock, Breton sailor T-shirt, your old gym shorts, Tony Curtis wearing a blazer and pretending to be Cary Grant in *Some Like It Hot*. Partner it with white or simply slice it with colors for a Riviera swish. Whichever which way you wear it, you'll wear it well and you will have them all standing to attention.

ও

NECESSARY VANITY

Newspapers and magazines seem to swing like a pendulum on the subject of vanity and, of course, it's a very convenient way of frightening, punishing and then advertising to women. At one level, everybody is excoriated for even considering Botox and face-lifts, yet on another, the pressure to look younger, more beautiful and to sip at the spring of eternal life has never been greater. It was recently reported that teenagers are beginning to have Botox. This is a tragedy.

However, if we take it as a given that nobody really wants to walk down the road in a pair of mismatched gym shoes, smelling of pee with a jumper on inside out, let us accept that necessary vanity should be equated with a sense of self-worth and secret confidence. Why shouldn't one look one's best at whatever age?

There are all sorts of health and beauty treatments that are non-invasive, life-enhancing and well worth investing in. As with so many things, the French have got it right: a good skin routine doesn't have to cost a fortune and reaps rewards over the years. The phrase 'because I'm worth it' has become something of a joke in recent years, but actually, you are.

(v: Bien dans ta peau, Moisturizer, Secret confidence)

ॐ

NETWORKING
(v: Dating, Get out of a rut and get involved, Instinct, Members' club, Mentors)

ॐ

NEUROSIS
(v: Exercise, Freud, Jung)

ॐ

NEVER TURN DOWN PROMISING ENCOUNTERS
We don't need to expand on this. Just don't. Life is short.
(v: It's a gift, Safety)

ೋ

NEW PEOPLE

Every six months or so the old address book needs oxygenating and new people need to be brought in. New people will keep you on your toes by offering fresh insights and unlikely experiences. Breezing new people into your life from all walks of life and from all nationalities is a great way to keep young, open-minded and full of zip.

(v: Little black book)

ೋ

NEW YEAR'S EVE

It can be brilliant or it can be awful and there is often no rhyme or reason why.

(v: Self-pity)

ೋ

NO SEX BEFORE MARRIAGE

'Abstinence is easier than temperance.'

– SENECA

According to the Greek author Homer, Hera, Zeus's much vexed wife, renewed her virginity each year in the spring Kanathos. In doing so she put aside the troubles of her marriage (Zeus was a renowned philanderer) and found sexual fulfillment again. In the twenty-first century 'becoming a virgin again' is a path chosen by young women who feel that in our oversexualized world the female sex has become objectified and undermined. They believe that by returning to the traditions of no sex before marriage one creates a space where it is possible to establish a relationship with a man, which is based on friendship, like-mindedness, respect and soul. They hope that out of this balanced and spiritual connection a true and long-lasting love will grow. This may well be the path for some of us but not necessarily all of us.

(v: Chastity, Entering a convent, Self-discipline)

∾

No strings attached

If you haven't had sex for a long time and somebody offers it to you, why not accept? No strings attached. It's a gift, not a life-long attachment.

∾

Not safe in taxis

If a friend's husband offers you a lift home, then proceeds to tell you his wife doesn't understand him, and lands a hand on your thigh you must blacklist him immediately and tell all your friends. The code is NSIT (Not Safe in Taxis) or MTF (Must Touch Flesh).

(v: Complete wankers)

ৎᠷᡪ

NOT THAT FRIENDLY BUT ACTUALLY QUITE NICE

Weirdly, the man who appears a little bit diffident and not very good at parties may actually turn out to be honest and proper and true, cf. Darcy in *Pride and Prejudice*. Don't rush him and don't dismiss him.

(v: Good husband material, Top table)

Office wife

It's quite flattering. A gorgeous man in the office who is happily married turns his attentions to you. Soon you are telling each other everything, going for lunch every other day and gossiping about work colleagues. All fine and dandy, but rest assured that he doesn't talk about you at home. Make sure you are still socially available to others.

(v: Cinq à sept)

Oily fish

Has got to be consumed on a regular basis to keep you clever, cheerful, slim and to keep your skin healthy.

(v: Eat your greens, Menopause, Skin)

❧

OLD AGE

"Growing old ain't for sissies."

– BETTE DAVIS

❧

OLD-FASHIONED ITALIAN RESTAURANTS

From the red-and-white tablecloths and raffia-clad Chianti bottles to the flirtatious patron straight from central casting who loves a woman who eats dessert, they're a great port in a storm. Gourmets may rhapsodize about crab and ground-squash ravioli, but OFIRs are guaranteed not to break the bank, and are ideal for tricky dates or impromptu work parties. We've eaten in OFIRs from Berlin to Thailand and they never disappoint.

(v. Ballooning weight, Carbohydrates, Gelati)

❧

OLD FLAMES

Don't go there. If you are still referring to them as an old flame, they are still secretly a live passion. However much you may think you have moved on, part of you is still hoping something will rekindle. We tend to revisit old flames out of boredom, pique, to make someone else jealous or to prove to ourselves how 'over' it we are. (If we were genuinely over it, they would have become our good friends twenty years ago.) There's nothing worse than sitting in the cinema with an OF thinking: 'We'll never be in the dark, just the two of us, again.' Or noticing a new item in their wardrobe that the new lover picked out. Yes, revenge can be a dish best served cold: 'Heavens, now he's bald/bisexual/bankrupt.' But that just makes you realize how much time you wasted. Reigniting sex with the ex is a dangerous game and you may get your fingers burned.

(v: Complete wankers, (the) Ex)

ⱱ⳩

OLD LADYISH BEHAVIOR

Being trapped in a routine and doing pedantic things with tea are quite old ladyish and should be avoided. As should overapplication of lipstick without a liner, and having to wear glasses while attempting to take drugs. Endless rooting around at the bottom of vast bags (looking for glasses, phone or keys) and not being able to use the remote control are quite OLish and should be guarded against. The cure? Smaller handbags, skydiving or a road trip through Italy.

(v: Adventure, Climacteric, Handbags, Losing things)

ⱱ⳩

ONE-NIGHT STANDS

(v: It's a gift, It seemed like a good idea at the time, Mercy fuck, On the rebound, Twice is polite)

ოო

ON THE REBOUND
'To be rejected is the beginning of being free.'
– GERMAINE GREER

Don't bounce off the furniture too much or get married within the year but do what you need to do.

(v: Agony, Bachelors, Mercy fuck)

ოო

OPEN MIND

Keeping an open mind is an important philosophy. This is not an excuse for putting up with bores and boars. Sometimes your instinct is right. But it's healthy not to make snap decisions, or over-plan. Just see what happens.

(v: Down the rabbit hole, Not that friendly but quite nice)

ოო

OPENING BROWN ENVELOPES (THE BILLS)

God, it's boring isn't it? Some of us would rather walk up Snowdon backward carrying a hundred-pound backpack in the pouring rain rather than open a brown envelope, but it has to be done. Facing up to managing your financial affairs is essential for a happy life. Household bills, credit card statements and tax bills have to be dealt with and the sooner you deal with them, the better. If you are self-employed, ensure that you have a good accountant on hand and if you are desperate put the bills in the post to them.

(v: Finances, Grasping the nettle, Insurance, Making a will, Money matters, Pensions)

OPERA

And the undoing of women. With a few honorable exceptions, notably *The Merry Widow*, women tend to get a raw deal in opera. Whether it's Lucia di Lammermoor going mad in her tower, Camille in *La Traviata* dying beautifully of consumption (though all things considered in pretty good voice) or those poor nuns in Poulenc's *Dialogues of the Carmelites*, it's not looking good for the female sex. Many of the women in opera are archetypes: their stories encapsulate a history of women who have offered resistance to the male of the species, often with dire consequences. However, if you like the combination of exquisite music and high drama going to the opera is the ultimate treat. Everything is on a grand scale: the set, the cast, the music, the emotions and sometimes even the people. Unless you are extremely unlucky you cannot fail to come out moved, transported and perhaps irrevocably changed by the experience. And no excuses about the expense. Every opera house offers the most amazing deals if you put the time in, and opera is often broadcast through cinemas and is occasionally free.

(v: Entering a convent, Film club)

ॐ

OPPORTUNITY
Knocks.

(v: I won't, It's a gift, Middlescents, Never turn down promising encounters)

ॐ

OPRAH [ICON]
'You can have it all. You just can't have it all at once.'

ॐ

OPTIMISM
You can fake it. Even pretending to be optimistic and outgoing can make a difference – it only takes twenty-one days to create a new habit pathway in the brain. It's a better way to spend your time than waiting for your credit card bill. And certainly cheaper than trying to lift your spirits through alcohol or drug abuse.

(v: Opportunity)

ॐ

ORBACH, SUSIE [ICON]
'Fat is a social disease, and fat is a feminist issue.'
'The Body Beautiful is so distressing because it is an assault on mothers, particularly the mothers of the generation that tried to change the world and make it a better place for women. The

assault on them to get smaller and smaller and smaller. We were trying to get bigger and take up more space economically, politically and intellectually and every which way. One of the tragedies nowadays is that young women have no experience of being okay in their bodies.' cf. *The Beauty Myth* by Naomi Wolf.✑

ORGASMS (THE POWER OF)

This is self-evident but not just because it's a glorious feeling. A woman's right to enjoy pleasure during sex was a cornerstone of the sixties sexual revolution and it continues to be your right. It's about time it was enshrined in the constitution.

(v: Booty call, It's a gift, Le gadget, Mercy fuck)

✑

ORTHOPEDIC FOOTWEAR

We're in love with orthopedic footwear. From nurses' shoes to FitFlops. From Birkenstocks to MBT (Masai Barefoot Technology) trainers. The first designs weren't very aesthetic, but now you can get glittery sandals, jellies, boots and tennis shoes. Men loathe 'wellness footwear', of course – too practical. Not enough arch of the leg, no erotic tension. Sorry boys, get with the program: it means we can walk for miles!

(v: High heels, Legs)

ფ

OUTDOOR EXERCISE
(v: Adventure, Comfort zone, Handstand revolution,
Trampolining)

ფ

OVERSPENDING
(v: Debt, Money matters)

ფ

OVERUSE OF THE INTERNET
It's not where you are.

(v: Technology)

ფ

OYSTERS

Six of the best! Oysters used to be the food of the masses.
Nowadays, while not quite at the level of a can of beans, oysters
are an occasional affordable treat. Creamy and salty, served
with lemon, Tabasco or chopped onion in vinegar, you have to
down them in one. You either love them or hate them, but if you
are lucky enough to fall into the former category they are filled
with zinc (more per serving than any other food) reportedly
incredibly good for your sex life and are carbohydrate-free.

(v: Diet)

Pain

'Pain is life – the sharper the pain the more evidence of life.'
– Charles Lamb

(v: Age of bereavement, Agony)

Parks

The park is the great democratic space. Everyone deserves an expanse of green, a place to lie in the sun, read a novel, have a leisurely lunch. It gives you a chance to expand your worldview, look at sculptures and historical monuments, chat to strangers, enjoy local gossip. Even if you want complete peace, you're out of doors sitting alongside your community. Human beings need to feel the grass beneath their feet.

(v: Green living)

༒

PARTON, DOLLY [ICON]
*'If I ain't done it, I'm capable of it or I just ain't
got round to doing it yet.'*

༒

PASSING STUFF ON
That is, the good stuff. The favors, the rides, the dinners, the
frocks, and in some cases, the man. It's very green too.

(v: Bombshells, Karma)

༒

PASSION
*'Love is a fire. But whether it is going to warm your hearth or
burn down your house, you can never tell.'*
– JOAN CRAWFORD

'Love without passion is dreary; passion without love is horrific.'
– LORD BYRON

We all need passion in our lives. Great emotion makes us write
poetry and music, take risks, climb mountains, scale continents,
find cities. It's thrilling to be the object of another person's
passion. It's like being the heroine of your own private film.

(v: Film club, Music, Quests)

෴

PATIENCE

*'I am extraordinarily patient, provided I get my
own way in the end.'*
– MARGARET THATCHER
(v: Counterintuitive feminism, Deferment of pleasure)

෴

PEARLS

*'Pearls lie not on the seashore. If thou desirest
one thou must dive for it.'*
– ORIENTAL PROVERB

*'Perle, plesaunte to prynces paye
To clanly clos in golde so clere;
Oute of oryent? I hardyly saye.
Ne proved I never her precios pere.'*
– UNKNOWN AUTHOR

Pearl is one of the greatest literary works of the Middle Ages.
Scholars still don't fully understand the coded symbolism of
this eponymous poem, but what we do know is that this is an
elegy written to the poet's daughter.

The qualities that the poet associated with his 'Perle' some
750 years ago remain true for pearls today. They are singular,
virginal, beautiful, luminous and secretive and they reflect the
essence of the soul. Pearls grow when a grain of sand embeds

itself inside an oyster shell. Once harvested, they tend to go cloudy and dull if left unworn for any length of time but quickly begin to glow again once worn against human skin. Don't hold back! Real pearls are never vulgar and if you are fretting because gentlemen prefer blondes, all you need to remember is that pearls look much, much lovelier on brunettes, cf. Elizabeth Taylor.

(v: Godmothers, I can't afford to buy cheap, Oysters,
Playing it cool, Secret confidence)

PEARS

Everything's gone pear shaped, we apologize. Especially those of us with a petite top half and heavier bottom. But actually can't we rehabilitate the pear shape? Think luscious ripe green fruit, a tapering vase, or the curvaceous body of a cello, cf. Botticelli's *The Birth of Venus.*

(v: Shapes)

PELVIC FLOOR

There's nothing more irritating after a thirty-six-hour labor than the physiotherapist, usually with a figure like a whippet, who bounces into the ward to encourage you to start doing your pelvic floor exercises. However, she's right. You don't need any special equipment. You can do them sitting, standing or lying down or at the bus stop. There are plenty of discreet ways to tone and strengthen your pelvic floor muscles. Think of it as an upward and inward contraction, as an internal workout. Hold the muscles tight for ten seconds. Repeat up to ten times. As relationship expert Tracey Cox reminds us: 'Use it, or lose it.' It makes a huge difference to your sex life and can help prevent old lady incontinence and other gruesome age-related liabilities.

(v: Trampolining)

⦿

PENSIONS

Back in the day there was a notion that we would retire at sixty and live on a pension. Unless you work for the government forget it! You will have to work into your seventies and possibly beyond. The upside is that you will stave off Alzheimer's and be generally far more fun to be around and live longer. That's a pretty good upside.

(v: Accounting, Grasping the nettle, Money matters)

⦿

PEP TALK FROM A FIERY REDHEAD

We all need one of these occasionally. Maybe it's a useless lover, something not quite right at work or maybe you are just in the doldrums, but the fiery redhead knows that the only way forward for you is a to-the-point, five-minute long, pep talk. It smarts a little at first but the wounds will heal quickly and twenty-four hours later you'll be raring to go back on the razzle with the aforementioned fiery redhead.

(v: Bachelors, Cocktails)

༄

PERFECT MARTINI
(v: Martinis)

༄

PERFECT PUT-DOWN
'I never forget a face, but in your case I'll make an exception.'
– GROUCHO MARX

Nancy Astor said, 'If you were my husband, I'd put poison in your coffee'. Churchill said, 'If I were your husband I'd drink it'. You cannot store up perfect put-downs. They come unbidden.

༄

PERFECTIONISM
'Well, nobody's perfect.'
– *SOME LIKE IT HOT*, BILLY WILDER

༄

PERSEPHONE
Persephone's abduction and subsequent journey into the underworld and her mother Demeter's desperate search for her reveals, in a many-layered way, how we all have the potential to abduct from within. Part of growing up is to be drawn to the darker side of life. By 'abducting from within' we take a course of action, consciously or unconsciously – in Persephone's case by eating a pomegranate that symbolizes knowledge and sexuality

– which may appear to be against our best interests. By entering the metaphorical underworld we are forced to explore a much more complex path. The story of Persephone resonates down the ages and touches on many themes in women's lives including mother/daughter relationships, fertility, rebirth, growing up, marriage, youth vs. experience, male control, abduction and rape, depression, grief and loss and the symbolic and symbiotic relationship that women have with the natural world.

(v: Affairs, Benders, Drugs, It seemed like a good idea at the time, Jung, Self-sabotage)

~

PERSONAL CODE OF CONDUCT

When you grow up it is important to develop a personal code of conduct. You don't have to boast about it or use it to shame other people. You just have to stick to it.

(v: Courtesy, Good behavior, Grace, Mistress, Philosophy)

~

PETTICOATS

What is this retro item and why the hell do I need it? The answer – because your frock or your skirt will sit so much better on your hips if you are wearing one. Truly, your looks can hinge on this much misunderstood undergarment. An added advantage is that it's much easier to wear a scanty pair of knickers underneath. Many a blip can be concealed with a slip. That is a petticoat's purpose in life. Look out for a beautiful bias cut, made of vintage satin or silk and make sure the material drops rather than clings to you. Full petticoats with gorgeous thin straps are very enticing in a Felliniesque way. We suggest that you will need several as, unless you are incredibly well organized, they tend to be hard to find in the morning when you are running out the door.

(v: Allure, Have you got the kit?, Vintage)

PHILOSOPHY

The central tenet of philosophy – how to live a good life – applies to us all. Studying philosophy teaches you how to approach problems, view arguments from multiple perspectives and think around situations. It refines your ability to communicate clearly with others and articulate your thoughts in a meaningful way. It might even make episodes of *The Simpsons* easier to understand! It's never too late to distinguish between your Descartes and your Wittgenstein.

(v: Keeping an open mind, Personal code of conduct)

PHONE ETIQUETTE

There is a button on the cell phone called OFF and unless you don't mind being taken for a teenage boy game addict we suggest you use it. There is nothing more dispiriting when going out for cocktails with a friend than to watch them scrolling through their messages while you try to make polite conversation.

Always turn your phone off before entering churches, theaters, cinemas and concert halls. Copy your SIM card, or get someone else to (probably a teenager or maybe a godchild), otherwise when all your contacts are accidentally wiped out when you lose your phone you will go into deep mourning.

(v: Courtesy, Godmothers, Technology, Wild swimming)

PHOTO ALBUMS
'A good snapshot stops a moment from running away.'
– EUDORA WELTY

These days we're just as likely to record birthdays and weddings on laptops and cell phones. But don't forget the humble photo album. For over one hundred years it has narrated our individual and collective stories and contained our most precious memories. It offers a permanent record of family history – what we wore, what we ate, where we went on holiday. A photo album gives us back our younger selves and children and grandchildren love them.

(v: Memory boxes)

PICK-UP ARTIST
You only have to read Neil Strauss's *The Game* to understand the murky world of male pick-up artists. Strauss's most insidious weapon is 'the neg' – a back-handed compliment calculated

to momentarily lower a woman's self-confidence. ('Nice nails. Are they real? No? Oh, they look nice anyway.') There are two schools of thought on this. One is that it is undermining and makes women with low self-esteem miserable. The other is that it's a silly little game and anybody who tries to play it is a bit of a git. Neil Strauss sort of comes to this conclusion at the end of his own book too, which is why we secretly like him.

PICNICS

Cold chicken or salmon. Pain Baynard, cf. Elizabeth David. Box of Vietnamese salad. Hummus. Baguette. A cheese. Berries and cherries. Chilled water. Chilled rosé. A tartan blanket.

(v: Cooking, Hospitality)

PIERCING

Sorry, earrings are fine. But nipples, navels, genitals, they're a body part too far. The most common emotion is regret. A permanent hole as a reminder of something we've changed our minds about. Think what you were wearing five years ago. Would you be seen dead in it now? Also watch out for mullets and men wearing slogan T-shirts.

(v: Regrets, Tattoos)

PILATES

It's all about 'the core' although most of us are blissfully unaware that we have one. It's too easy to slump in a chair, letting our stomach muscles collapse, or lean forward so we get that tell-tale 'old lady' curve of the spine, which also results in back pain and rounded shoulders.

(v: Yoga)

PLAY

'We don't stop playing because we grow old; we grow old because we stop playing.'
– GEORGE BERNARD SHAW

PLAYERS (HOW TO SPOT THEM)

Would-be players spend a great deal of time casually dropping the names of rich people, the names of artists who rich people think are cool, the names of expensive holiday destinations that rich people go to and the sums of money they have recently spent acquiring 'art'. It's incredibly boring but because you are well brought up you have to appear to listen with interest. True players just get on with it.

(v: Bores, Emergency exits)

⌇

Playing it cool

'Cool'– according to the rule books, you either have it, or you don't. At 20 you will not totally understand what cool really stands for . . . by the time you are 50 it's a mass of infinitesimal incremental changes in the way you think about life.

The appearance of a calm exterior, poise and self-confidence, even while your stomach is churning, will garner you respect and admiration. Remember, sometimes you have to act it to become it.

(v: Allure, Elegance)

⌇

Pleasure of work

'Work is much more fun than fun.'
– Noël Coward

'Choose a job you love and you will never have to work a day in your life.'
– Confucius

We spend most of our lives at work – so the difference between getting it right and wrong is life-changing. This is just as true for those engaged in unpaid work, such as caring for children or elderly relatives. A satisfying job can bring structure and meaning to life, along with mental and emotional stimulation. Ideally, we should choose work that lets us use the qualities we value every day, that fits with our 'Big Idea' of ourselves. Put simply, the best career advice is to find out what you like doing best and get someone to pay you for doing it.

(v: Money matters, Portfolio careers)

POETRY

If in doubt forget sex and discover poetry. Keep a slim volume of verse in your handbag at all times. Useful for queues, bus journeys and doctors' waiting rooms. But if you absolutely insist on fiddling with your cell phone instead, install Shakespeare sonnets as an app.

(v: Queuing)

POKER

Traditionally a male preserve but women are proving themselves to be extremely good at this game, cf. Victoria Coren. Not least because of the psychological double-bluffing required. Old-fashioned math helps too and, even if advanced algebra escapes them, most women are secretly good at adding 2+2. If you have a proclivity for card games (a childhood grounding in Crazy Eights and Gin Rummy helps) seek out a poker game near you. You will form a whole new bunch of eclectic friends, more than likely set up a regular poker night and have enormous fun. Poker skills are also translatable to other walks of life and will come in useful if you are on a bender and down to your last dollar.

Weirdly, having had slightly too much to drink may enhance your poker skills rather than lessen them. However, set yourself realistic financial limits and quit while you're ahead.

(v: Benders, Cheating, Counterintuitive feminism, Lazy math girl)

எஸ்

POLITICS

Our vote was hard won, and it is the duty of every woman to care about who is running their country. You may disagree with all of them (including the women) and elect not to vote, but then become a conscientious objector and spoil your vote. It will still be counted.

(v: Demonstrations, Lipstick, Very public inconvenience)

எஸ்

PORNIFICATION

Has become increasingly hardcore and accessible. The objectification of porn stars and prostitutes is relatively new and it is a gruesome by-product of the Internet, and an unpleasant aspect to the liberal agenda. At the extreme end pornography endorses submission and violence toward women through brutal and often depraved acts, which is totally unacceptable.

Porn stars often have drastic surgery to enhance breasts, reduce waists and slim thighs. In addition, the uniformity of the Brazilian means that these women are often totally hair-free. The kind of body paradigm this sets up is a sad male fantasy and one of the knock-on effects of exposure to online pornography is that boys and men have completely unrealistic expectations when it comes to a real-life woman.

Most worryingly, we've heard disturbing stories of young men surfing the Internet for porn, who see only hairless models and are therefore surprised to discover that young women have pubic hair. This is reminiscent of John Ruskin, who was reportedly so shocked by his wife's body hair on their wedding night that the marriage was never consummated and subsequently annulled.

(v: Hairiness, Pornography)

༨

PORNOGRAPHY

'Porn is not sex but in fact a very elaborate form of avant-garde performance art.'
– BIDISHA

Our advice is never allow yourself to be filmed.

༨

PORTFOLIO CAREERS

Many of us will work for life because we just can't afford to quit our jobs. Or we're just plain rubbish with money (preferring jam today and every day!). The good news: we stay engaged and active and society benefits from our experience. The bad news: no sun loungers in the Mediterranean. Which is why it's so important to set in place now the building blocks for a late career we can actually bear (not necessarily office-based). Maybe a two to three days a week consultancy, or a mix of PR, retailing, writing, entertaining, etc. Ask yourself what gives you pleasure, then how can you persuade someone to pay you for that? By definition, we'll be pitching to competitive, younger people – but actually everyone likes reliable colleagues who aren't after their job!

(v: Freelance, Grasping the nettle, Pensions, Pleasure of work)

လက္ခ

POSH PANTS
(v: Adventure, Camiknickers)

လက္ခ

POSSESSION

We can be possessed by the strangest of things: lovers, shoes, bags, gardens, cats, diamonds, you name it. It's great to have a driving force that pushes us through life. Part of the fun is that you shift your life balance slightly to adjust it to your current enthusiasm – but when your passion tips into an obsession warning bells start ringing.

Maybe we were going through a barren patch in our life, but if the love object appears to be Jeffrey from accounts, maybe it's a wake-up call. Alternatively, maybe it's just a temporary excuse to forget about our health and/or about our finances. Think of it as a holiday with a return ticket.

(v: Midlife crisis, Passion, Quests)

∾

POSTNATAL DEPRESSION

You may have had the easiest of childbirths and you may love your baby to bits but you can still succumb to postnatal depression. The symptoms of extreme tiredness, weepiness and loss of self-confidence often come postchildbirth and can tip into postnatal depression, which is a chemical malfunction exacerbated by hormonal changes and extreme fatigue. The health care system is extremely good at offering support to new mothers. Seek help.

(v: Blues, Childbirth, Depression, Meds)

∾

POWER

'Nobody gives you your power. You just take it.'
– ROSEANNE BARR
'Let's not take ourselves too seriously.'
– QUEEN ELIZABETH II

*(v: Deferment of pleasure, Orgasms, Power of prayer,
Power of weeping on the sofa, Secret confidence)*

∾

POVERTY

'Who, being loved, is poor?'
– A WOMAN OF NO IMPORTANCE, OSCAR WILDE

(v: Debt, Money matters)

ฅฆ

(The) Power of now

*'The eternal present is the space within
which your whole life unfolds, the one factor that remains
constant. Life is now. There was never a time when your life
was not now, nor will there ever be.'*

– The Power of Now, Eckhart Tolle

ฅฆ

(The) Power of prayer

*'The function of prayer is not to influence God, but rather to
change the nature of the one who prays.'*

– Søren Kierkegaard

The power of prayer is the power of hope over negativity. Just
be calm in the knowledge that a little prayer will make you a
sweeter person and could mean a great deal to someone else.

(v: Cancer buddy, Hope)

ฅฆ

(The) Power of weeping on the sofa

Sometimes we don't have to buck up and deal with all that life
throws at us. Lying crying on the sofa is exactly what's required.
You can indulge yourself completely for a day or two – and
get the whole damn thing out of your system. Forget a stiff
upper lip or keeping busy. Take time off work: allow yourself
compassionate leave. Life has dealt you an unfair blow. If you

reenter the world too soon, you'll regret it. Like a wounded animal, it's good to lie down somewhere quiet to grieve. Allow yourself any vice that helps – violet creams, bad TV, and the occasional whisky (for shock). Gradually, through the gloom, you'll be able to think about things properly and eventually reengage with the world.

(v: Crisis, Divorce, Grief)

❧

Pregnancy
(v: Breast-feeding, Contraception, Childbirth, Childfree, Fertility, Mommy bores, Termination)

❧

Present drawer
You need to keep a present drawer stocked with bottles of scent, luxurious knickers, vintage china and general knick-knackery to give as tokens of your esteem to family and friends throughout the year. You like to receive. We all like to receive, but giving is even better and very fashionably twenty-first century.

❧

Prethreaded needles
Extraordinarily useful.

(v: Department stores, Make do and mend)

ᴖ

PRIVACY
(v: Boundaries, Beach huts, Bolt-holes, Codependency)

ᴖ

PROBLEM SOLVING
'... tomorrow is another day.'
– *GONE WITH THE WIND*, MARGARET MITCHELL

Things always look far worse at 3 a.m. Give yourself permission to go back to sleep, 'It is the middle of the night, I can't solve it now', and tackle it in the morning. If you can put the problem to one side, instead of gnawing at it like a dog with a bone, a solution may come to you unbidden.

(v: Crisis, Lateral thinking, Power of weeping on the sofa)

ᴖ

PROPHETS
We are all drawn to charismatic teachers and leaders but remember even prophets can have feet of clay. You friend's hot new guru/meditation master/psychotherapist may well be bearded Dave from next door. Beware of false promises. If something seems too good to be true, it probably is.

(v: Astrology)

ça

PROSTITUTION (MALE AND FEMALE)

Anyone buying sex reduces another human being to a commodity. We all understand loneliness, frustration, the desire to separate sex from love. Clients may tell themselves it's a pretend girlfriend or boyfriend, a casual date, not business-like or mechanical. But prostitution is about money – and control – over another (usually vulnerable) person. The pro-prostitution lobby may argue that a woman/man selling sex is just selling labor (paying the rent) like any other worker, but we should not pretend it is a career choice. Violence in the 'workplace' is a daily issue for many prostitutes, not the extraordinary event it is for others. Of course sex workers deserve to be safe. Pushing the sex trade further underground is counterproductive: forcing women to work alone makes the legal activity of selling sex a much more dangerous business. But buying another human being – paying someone to act out your fantasy – is capitalism at its ugliest. For every high-end call girl, such as Belle du Jour, making a good living, there's a trafficked woman from Eastern Europe living in fear. In the end there's only one question: would you be happy for your daughter/son/sister/brother to do it?

(v: It seemed like a good idea at the time)

ça

PROTECT YOUR CORE

(v: Boxing, Pilates, Trampolining, Yoga)

ॐ

PUBLIC DISPLAYS OF AFFECTION

It can be extremely irritating to be forced to watch people oblivious to the external world exchanging bodily fluids six inches away from your nose. You probably long to shout 'Get a room!'. The rule of thumb is that hand-holding, hugging and general loving closeness is okay – anything else is too much but you must forgive first-time Romeo and Juliets everything.

(v: Affairs)

ॐ

PUDENDA

Sadly, pudenda is the Latin word for 'that which is shameful.' However, times have changed, be proud of yours.

(v: Hairiness)

ॐ

PUNCTUALITY

Is the courtesy of kings.

(v: Lateness)

✑

(THE) PURSUIT OF LOVE

'If thou remember'st not the slightest folly. That ever love did make thee run into, Thou hast not loved."
– *AS YOU LIKE IT*, II. IV., WILLIAM SHAKESPEARE

(v: Affairs, Booty calls, Cinque à sept, It seemed like a good idea at the time, On the rebound)

✑

PUTTING OUT FIRES

From the unauthorized overdraft to the meeting that never got rescheduled, we need to put out fires before they spread. It's important to stay solution-oriented, rather than wallowing in the problem.

(v: Grasping the nettle, Opening brown envelopes)

(The) Queen [icon]

Is without vanity, loves corgis and horse racing and has a personal code of conduct, which we only have glimpses of but is impressively old-school. She has fully accepted her destiny. We can say that very few others have.

(v: Icons, Personal code of conduct)

Quests (this has nothing to do with laser swords)
'Come on. We're all on one.'
– Joseph Campbell

Whether we are in search of a man/woman/job/car/higher spiritual plain, most of us have usually got at least three quests on the go. They feel like a cross between a crush and a prayer. It's personal and intense. Perhaps your quest is to have kids – or if you have them, maybe it's to look after them as well as you can. Or maybe it's achieving something such as staying off the booze or perhaps it's keeping your herbaceous borders bushy (as it were). But whatever they are, and however many you have got, we implore you to embrace them. Your inner quests are the motor within. Quests are what drive us and keep us going. They are the sign that we remain ready for adventure and what could be more life-changing than that?

(v: Adventure, Crushes)

⁓

QUEUING

You will have to sometimes stand in line and it is a drag but it is also our continued ability to queue that makes us proud to be human. Carry a slim volume of verse or a short but perfectly formed novel (*The Turn of the Screw*, *The Great Gatsby*, *To the Lighthouse*) with you at all times. This will ease the pain and distract you from the melee.

(v: Poetry)

RAIN

'Millions long for immortality who do not know what to do with
themselves on a rainy afternoon.'
– *ANGER IN THE SKY*, SUSAN ERTZ

Do not to be afraid to go out in the rain. Rain will not poison you and nor will it shrink you (sadly!). It is claimed that the beautiful bloom of the classic complexion is enhanced by rain. There is no need to make a song and dance about rain. Just get outside. If you have children, the school run still goes on. If you have a dog, he needs to ramble. So scarves on, put your gloves in your pocket, umbrellas at the ready! Life goes on.

(v: Blues, Depression, Self-pity)

ৎৰ

RAISING BOYS ON YOUR OWN

It's a challenge but above all you mustn't continue the battle of
the sexes that was initiated with their father with them. Try and
be empathetic, however difficult that may seem. Do not quash
their innate masculinity even if you find it baffling at times and
encourage conversation even if you only get series of grunts in
return. Encourage as much activity as possible. Boys need to
be run ragged as it gives them less time to get up to mischief.
Check pockets regularly and if you find anything untoward,
i.e. drugs or knives, discuss it openly, preferably with backup.
Finally, if the father is truly absent, call on a godfather (or
significant male presence) for help. Now is the time for them to
help out. Encourage cooking and other household chores, there
are plenty of male role models in that department, and this will
ensure that your boys can look after themselves properly as
they grow older and not become a burden to their girlfriends.
If they are old enough to have sex they are perfectly capable
of putting their jeans in the washing machine. Don't worry
if their rooms are ridiculously untidy. They have to live with
the mess, you can just shut the door on it. Litter the flat or
house with newspapers and inspiring reading material – if boys
can keep the reading habit through the early teens then they
will be readers for life. Once they are properly in their teens
encourage discussion and debate about setting boundaries,
timekeeping, attending meals, getting up for school and being
courteous. After all they live in a democracy so prepare them

for it. Most important of all, prepare for battle if they display sexist behavior toward anybody, but most of all you. Good luck.

(v: Brothers, Family therapy)

✌

RANTING

You don't find your topic, it finds you. One day in the middle of discussing real fur/natural childbirth/private education/the e-book vs. print, you realize you've been declaiming wildly for the past ten minutes. Ranting is great fun: it shows you're engaged, that you care. People enjoy watching someone in full flow. The topic can be as highbrow or trivial as you like. The whole point is to look eccentric. It's perfectly fine to punctuate your flow of words with, 'Sorry, I'm ranting' and just carry on. But do watch that you're not becoming an adult bore. If your friend's grin is starting to look a little fixed, stop.

(v: Bores, Old ladyish behavior)

✌

RAPE

Is not about sex. It is about power and it is usually perpetrated by men who feel powerless or who wish to exert power over women in order to feel that they are in control.

❧

READING GROUPS

There is often more than a whiff of competition about being part of a book group, although recent evidence claims that joining a group brings the same level of happiness as a pay raise. You may well discover that your readers are far too busy checking out your chintz, your wine rack and everyone else in the room to deign to discuss *Madame Bovary*. That said, it really is an excellent incentive to get books read and, if you are a passionate reader, to share your enthusiasm with others. If in doubt, start your own but pick fellow members carefully. Ban all conversation about partners, children, schools, holidays, houses or money and if your time and money are under pressure stick to wine and cheese.

(v: Film clubs)

❧

REGRETS

We've had a few.

(v: Benders, Drunk-dialing, It seemed like a good idea at the time)

❧

REJECTION

There are no two ways of looking at this. It is extremely hard to be dumped by a lover or sacked by your boss. It's a shock. It's painful. It can evoke long-held memories of grief and loss.

The natural impulse is to seek revenge and then, once we have calmed down, justice.

(v: Crisis, Power of weeping on the sofa)

◦◦◦

RELATIONS

(v: Brothers, Extended families, Daughters, Family, In-laws, Mothers, Sisters, Sons, Stepmothers, Teenagers)

◦◦◦

RELATIVITY

'When you sit with a nice girl for two hours, it seems like two minutes. When you sit on a hot stove for two minutes, it seems like two hours. That's relativity.'

– ALBERT EINSTEIN

Oh. Ok. We get it.

(v: Lazy math girl, Philosophy)

◦◦◦

RETIREMENT

Because the world is financially screwed very few of us are going to be able to retire. But we can still rejoice as we will remain connected to the world, live much longer and still be able to take taxis, cf. Diana Athill [icon].

(v: Deferment of pleasure, Money matters, Pensions)

ᘀᕔ

REWARDS

Rewards come when you least expect them. You're trying to keep faith in the darkest hour. Nothing. Still nothing. Then suddenly bang – the universe sends you an e-mail offering you the chance of a new job/holiday/assignment. Good fortune is mercurial. But it nearly always comes from taking a risk and breaking your everyday patterns – befriending someone, going that extra mile – without any thought of recompense.

(v: Karma, Where's my fucking pony?)

ᘀᕔ

ROLE MODELS

(v: Angelou, Maya; Blaize, Immodesty; Del Conte, Anna; Mantel, Hilary; Minogue, Kylie; Mirren, Helen; Parton, Dolly; Queen, the; Rowling, J. K.; Smith, Patti; Streep, Meryl; Suu Kyi, Aung San; Swinton, Tilda; Thompson, Emma; Westwood, Dame Vivienne)

ROWLING, J. K. [ICON]
'When you dream, you can do what you like.'

SAD

Though unattractively titled Seasonal Affective Disorder, this form of misery due to long dark winters can be banished by a cheery, disco-tastic, invigorating lightbox. Away joint pain, overeating, lethargy and carbohydrate dependency. At the flick of a switch, hello bouncy, fizzy invigorated individuals with boosted levels of serotonin and melatonin, which are stimulated through light. Every home shall have one soon.

(v: Carbohydrates, Diet)

SAFE SEX

(v: Contraception, Safety)

SAFETY

It's horrible to stop a woman doing anything, walking anywhere, suggesting limits on her freedom. But the number one rule is to stay safe. Always wait for the bus or train in a well-lit place near other people if possible. Walk the route you know best and stick to well-lit, busy streets. Look confident. If you think you are being followed, take action. The most important thing is you get to do what you want to – when you want to – without letting an idiot ruin your day.

(v: Adventures, Comfort zone, Dating sites, Long-haul travel, Strenuous exercise)

SALAD DAYS

'. . . my salad days,
When I was green in judgement, cold in blood.'
– *Antony and Cleopatra*, I. v., William Shakespeare

We are all allowed three great loves in the space of one lifetime. Despite the knowledge that our salad days are over and despite the onset of wrinkles and widening hips, late love offers us the chance of romantic fulfillment one last time. Late love has its own particular bloom and depth.

(v: Accepting invitations, Late love, Little black book, Open mind)

ϾᎧᔔ

Salary

At your annual review always ask for a minimum of a ten percent raise.

(v: Accounting, Money matters, Pensions, Portfolio careers)

ϾᎧᔔ

Satisficers (don't be too perfect)

'Satisficers' enjoy the pursuit of pleasure – but they know when to call a halt, or discreetly compromise – when everybody is getting exhausted. Far better to opt for the third restaurant you see ('This is good enough – it will do for me') than trail everyone around for hours. After all the point is to see your friends and relax over a glass of wine. The direct opposite of the 'Satisficer' is the 'Maximizer', perfectionist and driven, they are doomed to misery and regret, continually haunted as they are by all the choices that weren't made.

(v: Codependency, Perfectionism)

ϾᎧᔔ

Saunas, Turkish baths and spas

Spas are a crash courses in relaxation. Health insurance may cover them for a calm, collected life.

(v: Grief, Massage, Skin)

ᘒᔕᕋ

SAVING MONEY

If you can, save ten percent of your salary every month and then diversify your investments through property, stocks and shares however small your investment and tax-free saving schemes. However small your investment, seek advice from an independent accredited financial advisor.

(v: Debt, Money matters, Pensions)

ᘒᔕᕋ

SCARFOLOGY

From shawls and wraps to pashminas and bandanas – there's a scarf for every occasion. Pack one for holidays and it can double as a blanket, coat, belt, halter top, headpiece, even as a sarong. Guaranteed to instantly transform a dull outfit and rescue you on a bad hair day. Add a sparkly rhinestone pin or brooch to make a statement. There really is an art to tying scarves with élan. Think Bette Davis, Joan Crawford or Grace Kelly – who used an Hermès scarf as a sling for her broken arm.

(v: Animal prints, Jewelery for fat days)

ᘒᔕᕋ

SCENT

A great scent is the final link in the chain of your signature style. Seek out the classics. You will know when you have found the right one for you because everybody will tell you how wonderful you smell. Once you have found it, stick with it.

(v: Allure, Elegance, Luxury, Necessary vanity, Style)

ᏻᏛᎧ

SCHADENFREUDE

A German word that distills the feeling of satisfaction we sometimes experience at someone else's misfortune. It's not pretty, in fact, it's up there with jealousy and selfishness as one of the most ignoble feelings we may have about another human being, but it is a universal feeling and what's weird is it comes with a momentary sense of pleasure. Luckily, if you can put a name to it you'll find you can push it back into the box swiftly and no harm done.

(v: BFF, Frenemies, Freud, Jealously, Jung)

ᏻᏛᎧ

(THE) SEASIDE
(v: Beach huts, Bolt-holes, Infinite vistas, Picnics, Water)

ᏻᏛᎧ

SECOND MARRIAGES

Are commonplace. Enjoy them, celebrate them, but do try to ensure that you are not repeating the patterns of the first one.

(v: Good husband material, I don't)

ᏻᏛᎧ

SECRET ARMOR
(v: Elegance, Enigma, Personal code of conduct)

≈

SECRET CONFIDENCE

Some of us are naturally more confident than others but we all need to work on building up our confidence. The steady or quiet accruing of compliments, fulfillment through family and/or work, age and experience all help.

(v: Accepting a compliment, Camiknickers, Necessary vanity, Pleasure of work)

≈

SECRETS

'If you reveal your secrets to the wind you should not blame the wind for revealing them to the trees.'
– KAHLIL GIBRAN

Some secrets are fun, some are exciting and some are a downright burden. One person's secret is another's whopping piece of pernicious gossip. If you are the holder of a full hand of secrets, guard them closely, and do not place them in an e-mail. Very often you will be in possession of the equivalent of a little hand grenade, which you don't want igniting on your watch. Guard them carefully.

(v: Benders, BFF, Dancing with the devil, Gossip, Regrets)

వాూ

SELF-ACCEPTANCE

'The most terrifying thing is to accept oneself completely.'

– CARL GUSTAV JUNG

(v: Bien dans ta peau, Learning to love yourself, You've got to do it)

వాూ

SELF-DEPRECATION

Don't do yourself down. It's pointless and can become embarrassing and irritating for those around you. As much as you put yourself down they will politely feel the need to build you up and frankly that's not their responsibility.

(v: Accepting a compliment, You're the bomb!)

వాూ

SELF-DISCIPLINE

Is unfashionable but worthwhile.

(v: Diet, Quests)

వాూ

SELF-DOUBT

However great we think we are feeling about ourselves self-doubt seems to have an insidious ability to creep in and change the way we see things. It is like a worm gnawing an apple. It burrows deep and can be very damaging. It is not to be confused with useful self-examination or insight. Guard against it.

(v: Accepting a compliment)

ഗ

SELF-OBSESSION

Rather like being a bore (and the two are closely related), you are probably the last person to realize that you are becoming increasingly self-obsessed. Knock it on the head immediately. The signs are:

1. You are beginning to dominate conversations.

2. You repeat the same stories again and again, always about yourself.

3. You don't really listen to or take in what other people say.

4. You always somehow manage to bring the conversation back to yourself.

It takes a brave sibling or friend to point this fault out to you, whether in conversation or during a row. Your immediate response will be to feel cruelly hurt but please take this criticism on board and make some changes, otherwise you will end your days as a lonely old lady.

(v: Bores, Exquisite listening, Old ladyish behavior)

ഗ

SELF-PITY

It is fun to wallow in self-pity once in a while, but if it extends for longer than a day or two it can become self-defeating for you and boring for other people. However, you do need to take self-pity slightly seriously as it can develop into depression. So in the first instance: count your blessings and make a gratitude list, i.e. write down the ten things you are grateful for in your life. Do some gardening (even if all you are doing is replacing the plants or herbs in your window box) – a connection with the soil and the earth is apparently particularly therapeutic for women. Volunteer for some kind of community service. But, most of all, be easy on yourself. So, early nights, easy TV watching, wooly socks, etc. And, at the end of each day, think of two or three things large or small that you have achieved in the day, such as being nice to your neighbor's cat. If, after a week or two, you are still waking up in tears and/or none of your friends will return your calls, make an appointment to see your doctor.

(v: Container gardens, Depression, Gardens, Power of weeping on the sofa, Therapy)

SELF-RIGHTEOUSNESS
A really unattractive quality. 'He who casts the first stone . . .' and all that. It smacks of smugness, preachiness and boring self-obsession and if you continue down this road you will lose friends and alienate people.

(v: Bores)

SELF-SABOTAGE
(v: Persephone)

༄

SELF-SACRIFICE

Is not to be confused with being unselfish. Self-sacrifice has connotations of unnecessary nineteenth-century female victimhood. Your daily martyrdom – insulting to those who really do put themselves on the line – is boring for family and friends and probably ultimately pointless. Life may one day throw you an extraordinary calling, cf. Joan of Arc, the Fukushima 50, but until then take a balanced view of your needs versus other people's.

༄

SENSE OF SELF

'With stammering lips and insufficient sound
I strive and struggle to deliver right that music of my nature.'
– 'THE SOUL'S EXPRESSION', ELIZABETH BARRETT BROWNING

(v: Bien dans ta peau, Secret confidence, Self-acceptance)

༄

SENTIMENTALITY

Has its place but don't major on it.

(v: Keepsakes and talismans, Memory boxes, Tattoos)

 formula

SEX

'Sex is not a noun like coffee.'
– SYBILLE BEDFORD

(v: Affairs, Bachelors, Benders, Cinque à sept, Contraception, Exercise, Have you got the kit?, Instinct, No sex before marriage, Orgasms)

formula

SEXTING

The skill of typing your desires to the man of the moment and reeling him in for a nightcap at his place or yours.

(v: Sex, booty calls)

formula

SEXUAL ABUSE
(v: Daddy damage)

formula

SEXUAL HARASSMENT

An age-old male device for oversexualizing and undermining women, usually in the workplace, cf. *Mad Men*. Nowadays, there are very strict rules against it. Know your rights.

(v: Bullying, Politics)

◡◠

SHAPES

As an apple shape, you store your excess fat predominantly on your midsection and bust. Unfortunately for you, this kind of fat storage is known as 'android obesity'. It makes 'apple' the most dangerous of all body shapes, putting you at higher risk of hypertension, type 2 diabetes, coronary artery disease and premature death (compared to individuals with a pear shape, or 'gynoid obesity', where fat is deposited on the hip area).

An interesting and often shocking fact is that a waist measurement of over 35 inches for a woman puts her at high risk of all of the above diseases – so get your tape measure out! (You might want to check out any men in your life too – the waist measurement for men should be 40 inches or less). The good news is that apple shapes normally respond well to exercise and diet and you can very quickly see the results.

(v: Pears, Waist)

◡◠

SHAPEWEAR

Once upon a time curvy girls were laced into hideous fifties foundation garments, but today's figure-enhancing shapewear – tanks, bodices, T-shirts, dresses – is smart enough to wear as outerwear. The painless way to enhance cleavage, smooth out love handles and find that waist, which was last glimpsed in 1983.

(v: Ballooning weight, Necessary vanity, Waist)

ممم

SHECONOMICS

Just because you're a woman there's no excuse to be in debt. Be aware of how your emotions affect the way you behave with money. If you insist to yourself and others that you are bad with money, you probably will be. If you think you deserve to be comfortably off, that's half the battle won. Once you've worked out what's standing in your way, you can start to change your behavior – and attitude – toward money. A very important note to self is that your bank manager is not your father.

(v: Grasping the nettle, Money matters, Opening brown envelopes, Pensions, Something for a rainy day)

ممم

SHIPWRECK SCENARIO

The shipwreck scenario is quite a useful tool. If you find yourself high on life, whether it's a lover, a new job or a risky enterprise, focus a little on the possible downsides. A reality check is rarely wasted.

(v: Affairs, Crisis, Divorce, Househusband, I don't, Self-pity)

SHOES

The shoes, the shoes,
Won't change your life dear,
Your feet, or the shape of your legs dear,
Twinking away life like big Easter eggs
In the shiny shop window
Not for walking in you see.
Just wearing to a party.

– SARAH-JANE LOVETT

(v: Feet, Flats, High heels, Orthopedic footwear)

SINGLE SUPPLEMENT (WELL WORTH IT)

Yes, it's aggravating to be charged extra for single occupancy. Twin rooms are cheaper if you don't mind bunking up with a friend. But we'd argue it's well worth paying for bathroom privacy – and that vital hour alone to recharge before cocktails.

(v: Holidaying with girlfriends)

SISTERS

'*Whatever you do they will love you; even if they*
don't love you they are connected to you till you die. You can
be boring and tedious with sisters, whereas you have to
put on a good face with friends.'

– DEBORAH MOGGACH

'For there is no friend like a sister, in calm or stormy weather, to cheer one on the tedious way, to fetch one if one goes astray, to lift one if one totters down, to strengthen whilst one stands.'
– CHRISTINA G. ROSSETTI

No relationship is more complicated, more deeply tangled with highly charged emotion. The bond sisters share is dark and light, simple and dangerously complex. Constant yet ever evolving: sisterhood is a baffling incomprehensibility to those outside of it. And no matter whether it's taut and buzzing with daily contact, or slack and dusty from years of neglect, it's a bond that's always there.

The relationship you have with your sister is likely to be the longest of your life. Probably the most rewarding: she is a piece of your childhood that's never lost and the person most likely to stick with you in the future. So even if times are troubled, unless she's run off with your husband or bumped off your rabbit, best to forgive and forget. You are, after all, singing from the same song sheet.

(v: Brothers, Family therapy)

ट⌐ल

SKIN

'Eat an apple every day,
Get to bed by three,
Oh, take good care of yourself,
You belong to me!'
– 'BUTTON UP YOUR OVERCOAT', DESYLVA,
BROWN AND HENDERSON

Current thinking suggests that by eating an anti-inflammatory diet your skin will be kept in super-fine fettle. Well, what the hell is that we hear you cry? It means high protein and low-glycemic carbohydrates, i.e. not too much refined white breadstuffs and loads of fruit and vegetables. And lots of water, naturally.

(v: Diets, Eat your greens, Facial acupuncture,
Super-foods, Vitamins, Water)

ट⌐ल

SKINNY

As the distinctly odd Wallis Simpson declared, 'You can never be too rich or too thin'. Well, on some levels that may be true but it's not necessarily a question of choice . . . There are many women who are naturally very thin. This may be incredibly galling for those battling the bulge, but this is just the way it is. It is rude to go around endlessly commenting on people's skinniness and making them feel awkward and embarrassed.

(v: Diet)

SLEEP

We spend a third of our lives sleeping. It's a uniquely private experience even if we share a bed. The sensuality, the pure surrender (when we get it) is a wonderful thing. It's the brain's way of wiping the computer and rebooting. Sometimes creative problems solve themselves overnight. As actress Penelope Cruz insists: 'Sleep is the best way to happiness and beauty. Once, my sister slept for three days straight. My record is eighteen hours.'

Sleep can be a great refuge from difficult life events. Tell yourself not to reply to an upsetting e-mail or make a decision about a bad patch in a relationship for at least forty-eight hours. Instead go to bed.

Sleep makes us brainier (it helps maintain normal cognitive skills, like speech and memory). It helps regulate our weight (sleep deprivation lowers the amount of leptin the body produces, which leads to increased appetite). It's the fastest – and cheapest – boost you can give yourself.

Many high-fliers regard it as a waste of time and have accumulated a chronic sleep debt. But, like a bank account, make sure you pay in extra at weekends, or days off.

(v: Beds, Insomnia, Skin)

SLOE GIN

Should be in everybody's cocktail cabinet. Sweet and dry and a deep purple. It can be a secret ingredient in all sorts of jellies, trifles and fruit salads. It's brilliant with prosecco, known as a sloegasm, delicious with tonic or perfect as an after-dinner alternative to port. Or in the deep dark heart of winter sit around a fire and sip slowly, with pleasure.

(v: Booze, Dipsomania, Grappa, Hospitality)

⟿

SMALL TALK

Why do so many clever, high-minded people think they're too good for gossip? Scientists tell us it is fundamental to being human. It makes us healthier, boosts levels of progesterone (a hormone that reduces anxiety), and fosters trust and cooperation. And, in times gone by, gossip proved vital to survival, with the trading of tidbits helping cavemen catch thieves and democrats elect leaders.

Gossip is a completely different thing from bitching. It's when – over red wine or at the school gates – we begin to discuss how hard it must be if one person is more successful in a relationship. Or whether you expect sexual fidelity. Yes, we may mention a celebrity or two, but only to get everything fired up. You need to be interested in the minutiae of other people's lives, otherwise friendship or a romantic date can feel like a mathstest with more drinking. There's no let up. The big questions are lobbed over the net: 'Who do you think should inherit Pinter's library?', 'Did you read the new essay on Dorian Gray?' Bang, bang. Until you're pleading for mercy. No one can be that interesting or that well informed. If you want to become a great gossiper, you must:

1. Feign ambivalence.

2. Appear unimpressed upon receipt of gossip from other people.

To be blasé, in other words, is key. Be very Wikileaks about your gossip but never ever commit gossip to e-mail.

(v: Conversation)

ᴄᴠᴛᴀ

SMITH, PATTI [ICON]
'Never let go of that fiery sadness called desire.'

ᴄᴠᴛᴀ

SNORING

Let's get one thing straight, the fairer sex never snores. It's biologically impossible . . . unless, of course, it's a side effect of hay fever, feather pillows, dining late or hard liquor. That aside, snoring can be the great divisive issue in relationships. We all need sleep (anything less than six hours is dangerous). There are plenty of whizzy sprays and remedies on the market: surgery is a last resort. But whether it's your partner, best friend or you who's disturbing the peace, it's helpful to talk about it – and out the taboo. There's nothing wrong with separate bedrooms. You can read late and watch films on the laptop – and it can be damn sexy to visit each other's sleeping space.

(v: Ballooning weight, Grappa, Holidaying with girlfriends, Insomnia, Single supplement, Staying the night)

⇜

Snow

'I sought my lover at twilight
Snow fell at daybreak . . .
Secret or not
No matter.
Footprints have been left in the snow.'
– FROM *THE TURQUOISE BEE: THE LOVE SONGS OF THE SIXTH DALAI LAMA*

⇜

Soapbox

If you want to air your opinions, just do it. We've all got issues and how good it is to spread them around. Do beware, however, that you don't become a grade A bore.

(v: Bores, Demonstrations, Heckling, Politics, Ranting)

⇜

Sobriety

It is good to flex the sobriety muscle from time to time, even if this means going, 'Negroni? Water? Negroni? Water? Negroni? Water? Yes, please. A large double water, with a liver-boosting slice of lime too, please, Mister'!

January is traditionally the time when everybody gives up the bottle but it can feel rather glum if you and everybody else you know is drinking elderflower water round the kitchen table in the freezing cold. February has the virtue of being a short month. Lent is a good time for super sobriety, it has proper religious clout and, when you get to the pearly gates, St. Peter will have noted it down on your report card. Whatever your religious views, sobriety is a good way of keeping an eye on your drinking and calmly reminding yourself you can go for a week or two without. But, hey, everything in moderation. Including maybe this.

(v: Alcohol, Dipsomania, Quests)

Soirées

Are spreading through the country like wildfire. The formula is based on a perfectly mixed cocktail, a little music, a dash of poetry, a soupçon of a novel and some lovely drinks and canapés. Have an interval so people can smoke and chat, and a flat fee of fifteen dollars at the door should cover expenses.

(v: Cocktails, Film clubs, Music, Poetry, Reading groups)

Soothsayers

Are kind of fun once in a while, but dangerous if you become codependent. By all means read your stars, make your spells, magic your thinking, but don't spend too much time with a soothsayer as they can be awful drags and at the end of the day ruinously expensive – and we don't just mean financially.

(v: Astrology, Prophets)

❧

(THE) SOUL

Weighs 21 grams and is one of the cornerstones of religious belief, although its existence is generally denied by fundamentalist scientists. It's an amalgamation of genetics, circumstance, nature and nurture and the individual response to destiny helps to constitute this illusive core of our being. Friends and relatives often have a profound sense of a soul leaving the body at the moment of death.

❧

SOULMATES

Civil partnerships require you to become your lover's best friend and modern social mores suggest that this is a 'good thing'. But is this strictly necessary with your hubbie or your fella? Isn't it best to keep soul sharing for the girlfriends?

(v: BFF, Good husband material, Top table)

❧

SPENDING YOUR WAY OUT OF A DEPRESSION

Who'd have thought it? The Keynesian theory of economics suggests that we buy our way out of a depression. Now you have a proper excuse to spend your way through your blues. It's slightly unfashionable at the moment as we try and slash trillions off the national debt but like all good ideas it won't go away for long and, if your husband gets hold of your unfeasibly large credit card bill, just explain quietly and firmly that you are helping restore your country's economic fortunes.

(v: Money matters)

∾

SPERM
(v: Babies, Contraception, Skin, Termination)

∾

SPINNIES
'Don't laugh at the spinsters, dear girls, for often very tender,
tragic romances are hidden away in the hearts that beat so quietly
under the sober gowns, and many silent sacrifices of youth, health,
ambition, love itself, make the faded faces beautiful in God's sight.'
– *LITTLE WOMEN*, LOUISA MAY ALCOTT

The single woman is everyone's favorite caricature – whether demonized as home wreckers and ball breakers (and that's just the good stuff), or patronized as a controlling career woman secretly frustrated because they don't have a home life. But these days, singlehood is a state of mind. Sometimes you're in relationships, sometimes not.

Lots of 'singles' have grown-up children. People don't have to stay in bad relationships anymore, and women are relishing their new economic independence. No wonder the U.S. grassroots movement Quirkyalone promotes the idea that it's better to be single than settle.

And being a spinny has a noble pedigree. The first 'spinsters' appeared in thirteenth-century France as spinners and weavers of cotton and wool. The term denoted respectable employment, as unwed girls, orphans and widows forged a life outside the family home. In Victorian times, many middle-class spinsters enjoyed a life of 'single blessedness' (among them Florence Nightingale and Louisa May Alcott). Some taught, others set up all-female households. These special friendships would be regarded as loosely lesbian today, but no one worried much about female crushes back then.

(v: Cocktails, Friendship, Urban tribes)

SPITTING

'Stop it now, please', and spread the word, not the germs.

SPLIT THE BILL?

We're inevitably 50/50 on this. Yes, of course, it's important to assert your individuality, your economic separateness, your right to have sex with no sense of debt. But how wonderful, lovely and moving it is when a bloke says, 'I insist'.

(v: Courtesy)

STAFF

Behind every reasonably successful career woman are probably some staff. Don't exploit them. Pay them properly and recognize their worth.

(v: Alpha females)

~

STATISTICS

Tell you everything and nothing. The interesting thing about statistics is that they present themselves as fact but are usually governed by human motivation but without much insight. Distrust them as far as you are able.

(v: Spending your way out of a depression)

~

STAYCATION

You stay in and don't answer the phone and do exactly what you want for two weeks. The advantages are that you will save a great deal of money and won't have to go through airport security; the disadvantages are that you have to stay indoors at all times and can't even leave the house to buy a packet of cigs.

(v: Money matters)

~

STAYING THE NIGHT

It's easy to get old ladyish about this, but let's face it, everyone loves their own bed. However, it's good for us to mix things up. By all means travel prepared – toothbrush, lenses – it makes the appearance of spontaneity so much easier. Friends will supply the rest. Of course, if you're staying overnight for the first time, there are a few things to establish. Where's the bathroom?

Are there roommates? Does anyone have to get up early the next day? You might road test your underwear first. Ditto the condoms. But do try to relax, you're not planning to invade a small country.

(v: Contraception, Elegance, It's a gift, STDs)

ᴥ
STDs

If you can't get pregnant and/or are over 50 it doesn't mean you can abandon contraception. STDs are not just on the rise but in a mad rush to get to the party, particularly in the latter demographic.

(v: Condoms, Contraception, Safety, Sex)

ᴥ
STEPCHILDREN

It is unimaginably hard bringing up a stepchild, but however revolting they are being to you, try and put yourself in their shoes.

(v: Divorce, Family therapy, Modern families, Teenagers)

ᴥ
STEPMOTHERS

Traditionally stepmothers in fiction and throughout history have generally had notoriously bad press with a few exceptions.

Stepmothers are at the dark heart of many a fairytale, myth or legend and even the word 'stepmother' can still send a chill through a lovely summer garden party, cf. Snow White and the Seven Dwarves. However, perhaps it is time to reassess the stepmother. The truth is that in the world of ever-extending families you may well have one, be one or about to become one. The definitive book on the role of the stepmother has yet to be written so, in the meantime, it is worth understanding that this is a delicate and difficult role.

If you are about to become a stepmother you need to believe that you can be an entirely positive force in your new stepchildren's lives, while facing up to the fact that you are entering into a very complex dynamic. Your stepchildren may well be traumatized by events in the past and may unconsciously believe that the only reason you have power and influence in their lives is because you are sleeping with their father (which is sort of true) and that will feel very unfair to them.

You need to find love in your heart when there may be none; you need to create strong boundaries while being flexible too; you will need to accept openly your mistakes and, more importantly, that you are going to make a lot of them. There will probably be rows and you are going to have to learn how to make the peace. You will need to be scrupulously fair about money and in particular wills and, although it may seem counterintuitive, it is wise to encourage your husband to have as constructive a relationship with his ex-wife as possible. If your new husband is a widower do encourage open and loving and ongoing conversations about his first wife with the children. It may feel like a dagger in your heart, because stepmothers can begin to love their stepchildren very much, but this must be done with a loving smile on your face.

It sounds gruesome doesn't it, but don't wrench your engagement ring from your finger just yet. Please, please believe us that being a stepmother can ultimately be an extremely rewarding experience and if you haven't had children of your own, stepchildren can really be a gift from God.

(v: Childfree, Divorce, Family therapy, Modern families, Teenagers)

STICKING WITH IT
Don't give up too easily.

STRAIGHT TALKING
Instead of fuming and festering, why not speak your mind? And then be a grown-up and let it all blow over.

STREEP, MERYL [ICON]
'It is well that the Earth is round and we don't see too far ahead.'

ᘓᗷᖇ

STUDIO

*'Women, then, have not had a dog's chance of
writing poetry. That is why I have laid so much stress on money
and a room of one's own.'*

– *A ROOM OF ONE'S OWN*, VIRGINIA WOOLF

(v: Bolt-hole, Infinite vistas, Personal space)

ᘓᗷᖇ

STYLE

(v: Elegance, Instinct, Suits)

ᘓᗷᖇ

SUFFERING

(v: Agony, Aloneness, Freud, Grief, Jung, Self-pity, Therapy)

ᘓᗷᖇ

SUICIDE

To borrow from Nietzsche, the contemplation of suicide can
help one get through a long night. However, don't do it. It is
essentially self-murder and is devastating for friends and family.

(v: Crisis, Leaving the party)

ᘓᗷᖇ

SUITS (MEN AND WOMEN)

In the 1980s women had to wear power suits to prove they were
the equals of men. Dresses were considered suspect. The suit

said: 'Listen to me, give me your money and your votes.' It also said: 'I am an honorary man.'

Women's business attire has changed significantly since those Reaganesque times, becoming more relaxed and more 'feminine'. It's perfectly acceptable to 'mismatch' separates. The skirt suit can have a girlish dirndl or slick pencil skirt. Vivienne Westwood gives a suit a Lauren Bacall twist. Of course a great suit or tux, cf. Tilda Swinton or Carla Bruni, gives you confidence, skims curves and takes you effortlessly from day to evening. A string of pearls helps.

(v: Alpha females, Frocks, Pearls, Style, Whither feminism?, Work wear)

∽

SUNDAY NIGHTS
Have a particular kind of melancholy.
(v: Grasping the nettle)

∽

SUNGLASSES
It is rather like being inside a limo – you can hide tears of joy and pain, late nights and dark shadows. Whether you prefer classic Jackie Os or huge bug-eyed lenses, sunglasses play a game between concealment and display. Plus we are the lucky generation that's got prescription lenses. Just don't wear them indoors unless you're Anna Wintour.

(v: Elegance, SAD, Style)

∾

SUNSHINE
'Keep your face always toward the sunshine –
and shadows will fall behind you.'
– WALT WHITMAN

Get as much of this good stuff as you can. It keeps you happy, healthy and pretty. A sunny day can take all your cares away and it definitely takes your mind off shopping.

(v: Eat your greens, SAD, Vitamins)

∾

SUPER-FOODS
(v: Blueberries, Eat your greens)

∾

SUU KYI, AUNG SAN [ICON]
'Peace as a goal is an ideal which will not be contested by any
government or nation, not even the most belligerent.'

∾

SWINGING
The modern-day equivalent of the Dionysian orgy but without the attendance of the gods and it is once more back in vogue, cf. Killing Kittens. The phrase smacks of seventies-style sexual liberalism and a pre-AIDS age of innocence. It conjures up images of pampas grass and German porn but take stock, before

290- The Book for Dangerous Women

you throw your car keys onto the table, are you prepared to face the consequences on the school-run in the morning? Perhaps best left to the realm of fantasy.

(v: Affairs, Divorce, Tie me up, tie me down)

ᴄ᷎ᴧ

SWINTON, TILDA [ICON]
'Face slapped, fingers through the hair. Never look in the mirror, and never ask anybody how you look.'

Taboos
(v: Boundaries, Swinging, Tie me up, tie me down)

Talent shows
Avoid them.

Tango
(v: Dance, Exercise, Flow, Passion)

Tap dancing
Everybody loves it, but fewer people are doing it. Excellent for thighs, knees and ankles. Or, if you are feeling lazy, dig out some old Fred Astaire films and just sit back and marvel.

(v: Dance, Exercise, Flow, Passion)

∾

TATTOOS

Tattoos were once the preserve of sailors, fat ladies in the circus and the occasional aristo but now everybody has got one or is talking about getting one. Tattoos radically divide people and men tend to love them or hate them on women, they rarely take a neutral view. However, once again it's your choice and they can be a brilliant way of marking important moments in your life.

(v: It seemed like a good idea at the time, Keepsakes and talismans, Sentimentality)

∾

TAXIS

Never, ever, regret money spent on taxis. They can save you time, rescue your hair/wardrobe/shoes – or all three on a rainy day – and provide an important psychological breathing space in a stressful day.

(v: Safety)

∾

TEARS

Yes, they are occasionally embarrassing and a bore on the makeup front. When we cry the body releases toxins – such as the stress hormone cortisol – so you always feel better afterwards. Tears can melt the sternest of hearts and they can even incite an unexpected crush. True, it's hard for most of us to cry and remain photogenic. Lucky people can shed a single, graceful glistening tear while their already perfect bone structure is heightened by a becoming flush but most of us are chaotic, 33-hankies-a-day sorts, cf. Juliet Stevenson's fabulous portrait of snotty raw grief in *Truly Madly Deeply*.

As a rule of thumb try to avoid crying at work, unless in exceptional circumstances. Dig your nails in your palms. Take deep breaths. Walk around the park – or have secret convulsions on the stairs.

When you witness a fellow weeper – never more than five feet away in a big city – be compassionate. We've all sat on night buses next to a stranger sobbing (bad date, bad boss, bad everything), and felt anguished that we didn't intervene. Pat them kindly on the shoulder. Reassure them it's okay to have big, messy emotions and hand over some tissues. We all need to have a really good cry from time to time.

(v: Foundation, Grief, Kindness, Power of weeping on the sofa)

～

TECHNOLOGY

Is there an app for this stuff? Of course it's horrible, annoying and complicated but this is why teenagers were invented, yours or other people's, and jolly useful they are too. All those hours of downloading and poking and Facebooking and whatever else they get up to finally comes into its own when they apply their skills (unpaid, naturally) to your problems and needs. Teenagers love technology and are happy to help, mainly because it's much more interesting than tidying their room or taking out the garbage. It is second nature to them. They can whizz things around the Internet faster than the speed of light: it's a bit like watching Jamie Oliver cook pasta alla puttanesca. If you have to learn some basic technological skills, borrow the aforementioned teenager for a few hours. If you are really stuck, it's worth coughing up for some proper lessons from a trained adult. However, if you have fulfilled your godmotherly duties you may find your godchildren will be kind and help you out.

(v: Godmothers, Teenagers)

✎

TEENAGERS

Teenagers can be ghastly but the truth is 99% of the time, as the result of the rush of hormones into the body, they really can't help it. Don't enforce ridiculous punishments, i.e. cancelling pocket-money for two and a half years in a row, or prolong arguments because you are feeling hormonal and/or liverish. Once they get going teenagers do not have a turn-off switch. You do, so use it. Re: drugs, getting home late, sexual health and overdue homework, reassure them it is your concern for their health and safety that motivates you, not wanting to be a member of the moral majority. Re: untidy rooms, just shut the door and let them get on with it.

(v: Daughters, Divorce, Godmothers, Sons, Stepchildren, Stepmothers,
Tears, Technology)

သာ

TEETH

Time to invest in your mouth: it's never too late to rescue your teeth. And we're not just talking about fillings and gum disease. Smiling boosts your immune system, lowers blood pressure and releases endorphins (natural painkillers) and serotonin. It is a truth universally acknowledged that people with fabulous smiles are perceived to be more attractive, more intelligent, wealthier and younger.

Top tips:

1. Use an electric toothbrush. It's like cleaning the floor with a vacuum compared to a brush and pan.

2. Flossing (the 'f-word') is vital. Bacteria are clever creatures and they can hide in gaps between your teeth and multiply.

3. Use a straw. Fizzy drinks are bad for your teeth because they attack the teeth's protective enamel.

4. If your having a boozy meal, opt for cheese as dessert – it neutralizes the acid from alcohol.

5. If you know you will be drinking wine, brush your teeth before your first tipple. This removes the plaque that attracts the wine.

6. Eat sugar (sweets) all in one go. It takes an hour for your mouth to neutralize a sugar attack.

7. Grazing ruins your teeth.

(v: Necessary vanity, Secret confidence)

That's the way I always do it

Well, why not change it? There is nothing more boring than doing the same thing, in the same way, over and over again.

(v: Bores, Old ladyish behavior)

Therapy

Take your pick.

(v: Freud, Jung)

Things not to do in public

Picking your nose, clipping your nails, French kissing on the subway, shagging people on the escalators.

(v: Bad habits)

Things that make your life easier

(v: Bras, Cars, Contraception, Dishwashers, Family therapy, Friends, Frocks, Handyman, Lipstick, Lovers, Money matters)

Think like a man

'I would have been perfect as a man.'

– Annie Lennox

Research shows that men and women think differently but perhaps not as differently as you might think. So instead of wasting time on *The Rules* (frigid with a hint of peevishness), and who'd want to end up with the kind of man who goes for that type of woman anyway, or agonizing over *He's Just Not That Into You*, just think about it from the male perspective – whether it's food, sex, companionship, responsibilities or chores – and liberate yourself accordingly.

(v: Big babies, Complete wankers)

(THE) THIRD SPACE

Isn't to be found between your eyebrows, though pressing down with your thumb on this acupuncture point can help you ease tension on a busy day.

(v: Beach-huts, Bolt-holes, Libraries)

THOMPSON, EMMA [ICON]

'It's unfortunate and I really wish I wouldn't have to say this, but I really like human beings who have suffered. They're kinder.'

THREESOMES

These sound a lot more exciting than they actually are and one person tends to get left out and usually starts crying. But obviously you should try everything twice. Back in the day threesomes were symbolic of sexual liberation, but increasingly they have become the preserve of overpaid athletes and kiss and tell 'glamor models' and as a result, dare we say it, have become rather humdrum.

(v: Swinging, Taboos, Tie me up, tie me down, Twice is polite)

TIE ME UP, TIE ME DOWN

Once upon a time people thought bondage was quite daring, but nowadays as a leit-motif it's everywhere, whether it's advertising ice cream or a family car. A little 'vanilla sex' as the euphemism goes, such as being tied to the bedpost with a pair of silk stockings, is one thing, but it can get more addictive and extreme and before you know it you are in your own hand-luggage.

TIME

'You don't have time, you make time.'
– ANONYMOUS

TOP GIRLS

Alpha females burst through the glass ceiling for us – just to prove we can. They lead by example and rewrite the rules. They have changed the world with their determination and hard work, and they have made an impact with the way they live, or have lived, their lives. In general, they are self-created. But being an alpha female is not an excuse for bullying or machismo or hostility toward other women (or beta males). A truly assertive woman is great fun to be around. You flourish in her company and enjoy the ride (however bumpy) and because she is confident enough of her skills, her philosophy is that others should be too.

(v: Househusbands, Staff)

ᴄᴥᴙ

TOP TABLE

In the heat of the moment it can be quite hard to judge whether a man is truly worthy of your attention and love. Our suggestion is that you make a list of the men whom you would invite to sit at your imaginary 'top table'. They may be friends, lovers, husbands, fathers, godfathers, a bloke from the office, straight or gay. The key point is that although you may fancy them that is not the reason why they are welcome at your top table. Maybe it's for their moral values, maybe their intelligence, maybe their kindness or their courage in adversity, maybe it's for their genuine love and respect for women, children and dogs, whatever, but an unexpected outcome of this exercise is that you will remind yourself how many lovely men you know. Seat a minimum of six at your table and then ask yourself is there room for your prospective fella? You will be surprised at how quickly you come to a decision.

(v: Committed bachelors, Good husband material)

TRAINS

Hours of novel reading, great scenery, no fights or traffic jams. The sheer joy of surrendering to a train journey can't be overstated. As a car-obsessed nation, rail travelers are often regarded as second-class citizens but there's a huge romance to trains, whether you're embarking on the Orient Express or going home to see your mother. Book ahead and you'll get great bargains (two singles often cheaper than a return). Then spend the money you've saved on a swanky picnic or glass of champagne. The best bit – no one can boss you around or be a backseat driver – you're in charge.

(v: Poetry, Holidaying with girlfriends, Meditation, Never turn down promising encounters, Picnics)

TRAMPOLINING

Bored of the gym? Hate jogging? We are here to tell you that bouncing is far more fun. Trampolining helps you shape up and reduces cholesterol levels. It's the most effective aerobic and cardiovascular exercise for the whole body (a ten-minute session provides benefits equivalent to a half-hour run).

A word of caution: do watch drink-bouncing. Trampolines are for sober days. Most accidents on a trampoline occur when overenthusiastic adults come back from the pub and think: 'Ooh, let's try the trampoline!' Hours, if not days, in physical therapy can follow.

(v: Flow, Handstand revolution, Pelvic floor)

ოთ

TRAVEL

There is a new kind of snobbery along the lines of: 'Look how little I can travel with, aren't I marvelous?' When flying by plane, all this hand luggage stuff is fine and worthy, until you are freezing your ya-yas off in Dublin and your friend is trying to shove her running shoes into your restricted luggage. Our view is that it's worth paying extra to be able to take your luggage on holiday. If you are going abroad, you will want to take skin-care essentials, plus sun lotion and aftersun, and you will also want to buy stuff and bring it back. Yes. You will.

(v: Adventure, Balcony holidays, Orthopedic footwear)

ოთ

TRUST YOURSELF
(v: Instinct)

ოთ

TRUTH
'. . . to thine own self be true.'
– HAMLET, I. III., WILLIAM SHAKESPEARE

'And ye shall know the truth, and the truth shall set you free.'
– JOHN 8:32

(v: Guilt, Little white lies)

~

TRYSTS

We all know that lovely phase before a relationship becomes carnal – and you're still conducting the courtship out of doors. At this age it's important to have a list of trysting places. Chic, safe, low-key (preferably with excellent seating and shelter if it rains on your blow-dry), where you won't scare passing teens by holding hands.

The whole point of an assignation is there is a frisson of danger. You might decide to wear a splendid hat. But don't let things get too Gothic or self-conscious. Never take a new suitor to a place associated with memories of an old lover, it's just asking for trouble.

(v: Affairs, One-night stands, Twice is polite, It's a gift, Mercy fuck)

~

TUMMY TUCK

For many women when they hit middle age or beyond, some form of cosmetic surgery is now the absolute norm, but surely aging is not an illness – it's a fact of life? The emphasis should be about feeling great within yourself not pleasing other people. Medical science is changing so many aspects of our lives and also extending our lives way beyond the expectations of even a decade ago. Many women feel that cosmetic surgery is simply an extension of the opportunities opening up to them and therefore entirely a matter of choice. Interestingly, the men we canvassed on the subject were at worst indifferent to the notion of cosmetic surgery for women, at best quite opposed it. So, in theory, it is up to you but we do recommend that you do your research, cf. *The Beauty Myth* by Naomi Wolf, before taking the plunge.

(v: Facial exercises)

TWICE IS POLITE

Since the arrival of the Pill in 1963, casual sex has become part of modern life. Part of the fun is that in the heat of the moment there are no rules: the downside is that by the cold light of day, well, there are no rules. This can leave both parties floundering, uncertain and embarrassed and may, in the days to follow, lead to self-doubt and self-castigation. This is unnecessary. If we could all agree that 'twice is polite', i.e. once to do it and then once to get it right, the world would be a happier place. Alongside an agreement that this is not going to develop into a long-term relationship, this courtesy denotes mutual respect and appreciation. It could also be the basis for a long-term friendship instead (although we would suggest a bit of a break before contacting the relevant person again) and what could be nicer than that?

(v: Bachelors, It's a gift, One-night stands)

TWO CURES FOR LOVE

1. Don't see him. Don't phone or write a letter.
2. The easy way: get to know him better.
– *TWO CURES FOR LOVE*, WENDY COPE

(v: Drunk-dialing)

URBAN TRIBES

For many of us, friends are often our most significant kinship group. As we delay pairing off, end long marriages or strive to stay independent adults for longer, we crave the depth of knowledge of people who know 'the real' us: people who reinforce our sense of self rather than try to change us.

American writer Ethan Watters has dubbed the phenomenon 'Urban Tribes', an intricate community of people who live and work together in various combinations, perform regular rituals and provide the same kind of support as families used to do. Good examples of urban tribes are shown in TV programs such as *Sex and the City* and *Friends*, which show groups of friends who are always available for each other, a constant in each other's lives. One of the pleasures of living in the city is being able to see so many different tribes of friends, for the different parts of our jigsaw lives – from the school gate to sports chums to Friday-night cocktail friends. (All tribe members must be aware of the farcical elements of the others' lives.)

Every tribe needs a naughtier-than-thou friend – whose life is more rackety than your own. They might drink more, have affairs or stay out later. Whatever the vice, it's a pleasant reminder of your less well-behaved days, while imparting a modest sense that you really are quite responsible now. And, of course, we all have the high-powered friend – always running in heels, dashing back from somewhere exotic and on the way to somewhere you haven't been invited. The advantage: you feel connected to a different world. The downside: as soon as she's gone you feel like howling: 'Where did I go wrong?'

(v: Friends, Spinnies)

ↄ⌒

URBAN WALKING

You don't need specialist equipment – just lightweight sneakers you can throw in your bag. Building 'active travel' into your day is far easier than going to the gym or the pool. You can do it in an art gallery, the park or while shopping. Or rather like the Grand Old Duke of York and his ten thousand men, you can march yourself to the top of the hill and march yourself down again.

(v: Ballooning weight, Comfort zone, Green exercise)

Vagina monologues
'My teeth, my car, my vagina, my business.'
– Kelly Osbourne
(v: Cunt, Pelvic floor)

Variety is the spice of life
(v: Mojo)

Veins

No one wants to talk about this, but veins are not your fault. Weight has nothing to do with them, nor does standing for long periods of time, and neither are they a direct result of pregnancy. 'Veins' run in families. A little-known fact is that men are more likely to suffer problems with veins, although women are more likely to ask for treatment.

You don't need to suffer in silence. Forget the idea that it's an old lady's ailment. Surgeons say we develop faulty valves in our leg veins at an alarmingly young age. One in twenty eleven-year-old schoolgirls has already lost her valves, and one in nine has by the age of eighteen. The problem starts when the valves in your veins fail and thus allow blood to go back the wrong way down your leg, which causes the vein to start dilating. It is believed that it is the stretching of this muscle coat that accounts for the painful symptoms such as tender veins and apparent bruising. In the old days, treatment was brutal: veins were removed by stripping under general anesthetic, which caused bruising and required two to three weeks off work. In 80% of cases, they grew back within five years. The good news is we now have 'keyhole surgery' for veins. You can be in and out of hospital the same day and the recovery time is about two weeks.

(v: Legs, Necessary vanity)

ᴄᴠᴛᴧ

(A) VERY PUBLIC INCONVENIENCE

When Gordon Selfridge opened his eponymous store in London in 1909, one of its biggest selling points was the 'Ladies Room', which women would visit for its own sake. The creation of these toilets was a bellwether for women's rights and the fight for sexual equality. A lack of public toilets was an effective way to ensure that women stayed in or close to their homes. The arrival of the public convenience (how canny was Mr.

Selfridge?) acted as a nexus for a variety of things that helped women achieve equality, such as being able to ride a bicycle, a change in underwear and a relaxation of dress codes. The department store, in particular, benefited from the latter two developments.

(v: Lipstick, Politics)

VIAGRA

Let's not get into the details but if you want to have a satisfying sex life into your fifties and sixties it may be that your partner will need to take some Viagra from time to time. It has been said that it is like making love to a diving board, but we suppose there are worse things.

(v: Salad days)

VINTAGE

Wear a 1920s tea dress or edgy retro jacket and you have that dash of untraceable cool. No danger of bumping into someone in the same thing. Each piece has its own secret history.

Back in the day families passed on castoffs to relatives, not because it was chic – or even green – but because they were poor. As a result wearing hand-me-downs was humiliating. Punk changed everything, thank God, and suddenly it is cool to recycle, but the essential rule of thumb is don't dress in vintage head to foot, you may look too Miss Marple – but tweedy two-piece suits can be fashion gold. The trick is not to wear the librarian-worthy skirt and jacket together or if you insist make sure you are wearing fishnets too.

Buying vintage means you can be more ethical while enjoying your individuality. Second-hand has soul. In fact the new euphemism for used clothing is 'gently used' or 'love worn'. No longer a badge of shame – it's a badge of honor.

(v: Bobby pins)

VITAMINS

We all love stockpiling dinky bottles full of beta-carotene and selenium, but really we would be better off obtaining antioxidants and vitamins from fruit and vegetables.

(v: Eat your greens, Metabolism, Skin)

Waist (expanding)

If you are fashionably and boyishly slender don't bother to read this entry. If like most of us you are curvy of shape, looking after your waist is vital. Forget about dieting, forget about weighing yourself and just concentrate on fine-tuning your waist. A waist gives you shape, a graceful line and is for most men irresistibly sexy. All you have to do is find the clothes to match: nothing looks more gorgeous than a beautifully made corset on a woman with a proper waist. Looking after your waist also has some unexpected health benefits too. If you keep your waist trim you will, in due course, fend off dreary age-related medical conditions such as heart disease and diabetes.

(v: Ballooning weight, Boxing, Helen Mirren, Necessary vanity, Petticoats, Secret confidence, Vintage, Wear black wisely)

ભળ

WALKERS

Every woman over 40 needs a charismatic man she can take to parties who will laugh at her jokes and remember which cocktail she likes. You don't automatically sleep together (many of the best walkers are gay) but it might be quite nice if you did. Why shouldn't women who are between relationships make the same pragmatic decisions as men?

(v: Think like a man)

ભળ

WALKING AWAY

Sometimes this is the only thing to do if a situation has become untenable.

(v: Almost date, Bores, Emergency exit)

ભળ

WAR PAINT

Is just that. Remember that ladies. Go forth.
(v: Lipstick)

ભળ

WARD WEAR

Looking and feeling good is vital to getting you on the road to recovery, so bring on the ward wear. Gone are the days when a pair of slippers and quilted dressing gown would suffice. No girls, now you require an eye-popping capsule wardrobe of ward wear. If you are thinking airplane garb, along with socks (cashmere socks are ruinously expensive but if someone offers go for it), a throw to snuggle up in and some comfortable pants, if you are allowed to wear them, you are on the right track. You need something that you can both pad about in (stitches permitting) and lounge about in while you are recuperating, as you always need to be slightly on guard in case that sexy doctor (or nurse) pops by to see you.

1. Eye masks are good for sleeping during the day.

2. An iPod will get you through pain, boredom and hospital insomnia. If you haven't got one of your own, borrow one, and if a kind friend asks if there is anything they can do to help, then downloading a selection of soothing and soul-calming music is a useful task you can ask of them.

3. Reading. We suggest some volumes of poetry. Anthologies are good. Poems are easy to read in short bursts, particularly after an anesthetic when concentration can be affected.

4. An Advil, to de-puff your face and help lymphatic drainage.

5. Writing paper is essential. Now is the chance to catch up on your thank-you letters.

6. Don't forget scent and mascara. And definitely dry shampoo.

Ward wear is the last thing you will be thinking about as the dreaded day dawns, but actually once you are out of your scratchy paper gown it's important to look and feel as good as you can; you never know who might visit, so go for comfy, loose-fitting linen trousers.

*(v: Cancer, Childbirth, Hospital etiquette, Leaving the party,
Necessary vanity, Secret confidence)*

∽

WATER

Water is everything and we waste it at our peril for it is vital for all forms of life. It represents physical freedom, purity, cleanliness. In 1810 Lord Byron, despite his club foot, found his ultimate freedom and challenge in swimming the choppy five mile stretch of the Hellespont, where the Black Sea flows to the Aegean, and Asia almost kisses Europe.

Water comes with bubbles, or still: through waterfalls, via rivers, showers, seas and rain. It can pound you and quench you, drown you and save you, and you cannot exist without it. Drink it in throughout the day to keep healthy, stealthy and wise.

It can baptize you and anoint you. And as many a fair maiden knows, there is simply nothing like it for washing that man right out of your hair. Literally. Rumor is, it works.

(v: Rain, Seaside, Skin, Wild swimming)

∽

WEAR BLACK WISELY

Particularly when you are older. You don't want to look like a Greek granny, an aging Left Bank student or a backing singer for Iron Maiden. Think Fellini, then think pencil skirts and slingbacks, maybe topped off with a little cardigan, and you're away. So Anita Ekberg. Whatever you do don't bedeck yourself in black day in, day out. It's an easy trap because it feels fail safe.

The little black dress should be just that – little. Beautifully tailored hunting jackets are a good look with skirts or capri pants. As are cashmere wraps. Charcoal greys and deep dark purples are a little more forgiving on the crow's feet but a black pencil skirt gives you the perfect silhouette, so if it takes a pair of iron knickers or 'grippers' to pull it off, so be it.

(v: Color me beautiful)

✧

WEARING WHITE DRESSES

It's rare for somebody to remain a virgin until they get married so nowadays the wearing of a white wedding dress is a symbolic gesture rather than a reflection of a reality. Back in the day if you were marrying for a second time a pretty dress or sensible suit was appropriate. Nowadays you can go to town. Again.

(v: Catching the bouquet, Wedding cakes, Will you marry me?)

✧

WEDDING CAKES

What is fabulous about the way we live now is that we can still respect tradition but we can reinterpret it and bend it to our will. We've heard about modern wedding cakes made of cheese, jelly, profiteroles, sandwiches and digestive biscuits but the essential truth remains the same. A wedding cake represents abundance, fertility and hospitality and whether you cut it with a knife, a sabre or a cheese parer, the symbolic moment when husband and wife cut the 'cake' is when they open up their newly minted marriage to family and friends. Today's wedding cake retains its iconic status but reflects the diversity of modern lives. It's so cool to see same-sex grooms or brides atop the cake. Not all marriages last forever but 99% of the time a marriage is made with the very best of intentions. Play your part.

(v: Catching the bouquet, Wearing white dresses, Will you marry me?)

WELL PUT TOGETHER

Is a fabulous, slightly counterintuitive expression, for women who always seem to get it right. It means that the outfits are good, inspiringly arranged and either bang 'on trend' or foxily bohemian. It means that she knows how to sling together a certain bag with a certain high heel, and a particular print with a just-so fur stole. You wouldn't have necessarily thought of it but she has an innate originality, which means that she can do just that. She looks so great that you are happy to express your undiluted admiration for the fact that she wears it well.

(Animal prints, Elegance, Fur, Style, Vintage)

ریحא

WESTWOOD, DAME VIVIENNE [ICON]
*'I think people should make an effort every
single day to try to look special.'*

ریحا

WET WIPES

Easily and cheaply acquired, they are probably hideously
ecologically dodgy. However, from toilet seats (although we
promise you won't get pregnant sitting on one) to baby-sick to
dog poo (and that's just the half of it), they are unbelievably and
stupidly useful. If you have everything but the kitchen sink in
your handbag, you may as well throw in a packet of wet wipes,
just because you can.

(v: Babies, Boy toys Festivals)

ریحا

WHERE'S MY FUCKING PONY?

All of us from time to time have an overdeveloped sense of
entitlement.

ریحا

WHITE

Originally inspired by Queen Elizabeth the Queen Mother,
who wore white when she mourned her mother on a visit to
Paris in 1937, Coco Chanel loved a touch of white at her collar.
She knew that it throws light up to the face; making almost

everyone look as if they are in a picture painted by Vermeer. Linen sheets. Pure white walls brighten up your life. Just keep it all as fresh as a daisy.

(v: Beds, Wearing white dresses, Wedding cakes)

✍

WHITHER FEMINISM?

Where did feminism go and why has it become such a dirty word? Presumably it has overridden its jokey 'wimmin' satirical soubriquet by now. Shouldn't our deep, complex and poignant history be a key element in the educational curriculum for young women (and men) in the twenty-first century?

If the whole issue was really about good health care, equal pay and the right to vote, surely we need to pay more than a little respect to those who led the way – such as Florence Nightingale. And what about 'books as bombs'? Authors such as Simone de Beauvoir, Betty Friedan, Germaine Greer, Kate Millett and Andrea Dworkin drove the public debate about gender and were often pilloried and reviled in their attempt to do so. There is a long list of people we need to thank, so please let's not forget what they stood for, whom they stood up to, and how much we owe them.

(v: Hilary Mantel, Principles)

❧

WILD
'I'm not dangerous, I'm deadly.'
– ANITA PALLENBERG

❧

WILD NIGHTS
'Wild nights – Wild nights!
Were I with thee
Wild nights should be
Our luxury!
Futile – the winds –
To a Heart in port –
Done with the Compass –
Done with the Chart!
Rowing in Eden –
Ah – the Sea!
Might I but moor – tonight –
In thee!'
– 'WILD NIGHTS! – WILD NIGHTS!', EMILY DICKINSON

❧

WILL YOU MARRY ME?
This is the twenty-first century. It's okay to ask.

(v: Engagement, Wearing white dresses, Wedding cakes)

ᴄᴧ
WINE

There's a lot of snobbery about wine. You may be someone who knows your Fleurie from your Rioja, or just a 'one above house' type of girl, but a glass of wine marks the moment you award yourself a unit of pleasure. Sheer joy.

(v: Ballooning waist, Benders, Emotional overdrinking)

ᴄᴧ
WINTER

'Unseen buds, infinite, hidden well,
Under the snow and ice, under the darkness, in every
square or cubic inch.'
– 'UNSEEN BUDS', WALT WHITMAN

'When daffodils begin to peer,
With heigh! the doxy over the dale,
Why, then comes in the sweet o' the year;
For the red blood reigns in the winter's pale.'
– *THE WINTER'S TALE*, IV. III., WILLIAM SHAKESPEARE

Who doesn't love the first chill of winter combined with a bright blue sky or the joy of waking up to a snowbound winter world or the mystery of making a magic spell to celebrate the winter solstice? On the other hand, whose heart doesn't sink at the thought of waking up, still exhausted, in the darkness, and feel their spirits lowering when the street lights come on at 4 p.m.?

Winter, quite literally, can feel like our darkest hour and seems at times to be never-ending but don't forget that it's just a matter of time before the first crocuses come pushing up through the earth. Winter is when the world renews itself again – and you are included in that.

(v: Blues, Magic spells, SAD, Suicide)

WISDOM

'Wisdom is the daughter of experience.'
– LEONARDO DA VINCI
(v: Libraries)

WITCH HUNTS

The persecution of women through accusations of witchcraft has a dark history in the western world. But while women may no longer be drowned in barrels in fast-flowing rivers or burnt at the stake, witch hunts are still alive and well. The focus hasn't changed much. Generally a woman perceived as not taking a traditional route in terms of career, marriage or children can come under scrutiny and then find herself the subject of an obscene level of criticism. So next time you see a woman being hounded through the press, don't leap to conclusions, research the facts and, perhaps more importantly, the way the facts are presented and think again. If necessary, offer support via the web or any other means at your disposal.

(v: Violence against women)

〜

WOLF-WHISTLING

Being wolf-whistled at in the street can feel boring and undermining but in the new age of pornification, it has taken on an almost sixties, retro *Carry On* feel. Of all the sexist assaults, wolf-whistling has begun to be the least offensive and you may well miss it much more than you imagine once it finally stops.

(v: It's a gift)

〜

WOMEN'S MOVEMENT

The seven demands of the movement were . . .

1. Equal pay.

2. Equal education and job opportunities.

3. Free twenty-four-hour nurseries.

4. Free contraception and abortion on demand.

5. Financial and legal independence.

6. An end to discrimination against lesbians and a woman's right to define her sexuality.

7. Freedom from intimidation by the threat or use of violence and an end to male aggression and dominance.

❧

WORK WEAR
(v: Suits, Vintage, Well put together)

❧

(THE) WORST HAS ALREADY HAPPENED
Often the thing you fear most has already happened to you.

❧

WRATH
'Don't let the sun go down on your wrath.'
– EPHESIANS 4:26

'You are allowed quite a lot of late Sundowns.'
– ANTONIA FRASER

❧

WRINKLES
Some people hate their wrinkles and some people love them. Depending on your perspective, they are either the mark of your experience and the map of your life or they are the signifier of impending middle age and all the indignities that come with it. We recommend that you focus on the former.

(v: Facial exercises, Skin)

XYZ

XXXs

Spread them reasonably, liberally, but wisely.

YOGA

You've read enough about the benefits of yoga to last a lifetime, and maybe the next one too. Suffice to say it is 'a good thing', it comes in a variety of forms and there is probably a yoga studio (reasonably) near you, but don't forget yoga is a series of meditations not a quick-fix exercise routine.

(v: Ballooning weight, Waist)

YOU DECIDE

We all give advice and most of us seek advice and there is plenty of advice, whether you want it or not, in the pages of this book. But only you can decide.

(v: Accepting advice)

YOU'RE THE BOMB!

A fantastic Trinidadian expression that means that you are it, you make it happen, you are where it starts and finishes.

(v: Bien dans ta peau, Necessary vanity, Secret confidence)

YOU'RE ONLY YOUNG TWICE
'Life can only be understood backwards;
but it must be lived forwards.'
– SØREN KIERKEGAARD

Stop procrastinating. Stop making endless lists. Or telling people at dinner parties how you're going to write a novel/move to New York/start that lavender farm. We've heard it all before. And it's boring. You're the only grown-up in the room now. Just give it a go.

CREDITS

Quoted with kind permission from the following sources:

p.145 Copyright © 1945 by Nancy Mitford. Reproduced by permission of the Estate of Nancy Mitford, c/o Rogers, Coleridge & White, Ltd., 20 Powis Mews, London, W11 1JN

p.146 © Patrick Marber, *Closer*, and Methuen Drama, an imprint of Bloomsbury Publishing Plc, 1997

p.171 "Fashion, beauty and women's lives: the great debate," Emma John, 27 February 2011, Guardian News & Media, Ltd. 2011.

p.185 From *The Power of Now* Copyright © 1997 by Eckhart Tolle. Reprinted with permission of New World Library, Novato, CA. www.newworldlibrary.com.

p.215 *Status Anxiety* by Alain De Botton (Hamish Hamilton, 2004). Copyright © by 2004 Alain de Botton.